PRAISE FO
KILL THE DOG

Simply the best book on screenwriting ever written.
GEOFFREY THORNE
Co-Executive Producer, *Magnum P.I.*

Self-anointed "screenwriting guru" charlatans whose only experience is propagating bad advice, have finally met their match in Paul Guyot's *Kill the Dog*. This book is an instant classic!
RANDI MAYEM SINGER
Screenwriter, *Mrs. Doubtfire*

I've sat with Paul Guyot in writers rooms during late night emergency production rewrites and stood with him in the pouring rain shooting on location—for practical advice on screenwriting from a working pro, from script to set, he's your man.
JOHN ROGERS
Executive Producer, *Leverage, The Librarians*

Guyot is a scarred old pro, and his advice is real, practical, tested, and solid gold.
LEE CHILD
Internationally bestselling author of the Jack Reacher series

Paul Guyot is one of the best I've worked with, and with this book he has revolutionized the craft of screenwriting!
JONATHAN FRAKES
Star Trek Picard

This book sucks.
SOME GUY
On the Internet

KILL
THE DOG

ALSO BY PAUL GUYOT

SNOOPS
Higher Calling

FELICITY
The Love Bug
Truth or Consequences

LEVEL 9
Avatar
Ghost in the Machine

JUDGING AMY
RIGHTS of Passage
Boston Terriers from France
Damage Control
Looking for Quarters
CSO Hartford, Into the Fire
Sex & the Single Mother
Werewolves of Hartford
The Song That Never Ends
Sex, Lies, and Expedia.com

LEVERAGE
The Carnival Job
The Boiler Room Job
The Radio Job
The Blue Line Job
The French Connection Job
The Toy Job

THE LIBRARIANS
And Santa's Midnight Run
And the Apple of Discord
And the Rule of Three
And the Drowned Book, And
What Lies Beneath the Stones
And the Infernal Contract
And the Image of Image
And the Final Curtain

NCIS: NEW ORLEANS
Sins of the Father
Empathy

TALK TO ME
TNT pilot

THE DARK
TNT pilot

THE BLACK 22S
20th Century Fox pilot

THE JUMP
20th Century Fox pilot

49
Anonymous Content pilot

SUPERS
Imagine Entertainment pilot

BITTER BREW
CBS pilot

GEOSTORM

TIME BANDITS

NO TEARS FOR THE DEAD

THE BLACK 22S FEATURE

PLUS, A HECK OF A LOT
he wasn't paid to write.

THE FIRST BOOK ON SCREENWRITING TO TELL YOU THE TRUTH

PAUL GUYOT

Domestique, Inc. • Los Angeles • 2023

ISBN: 979-8-218-23854-4

Cover design: Desi Aragon
Interior design: Typeflow

for the biscuit, the bump, and the bun

CONTENTS

PREFACE

I LOVE DOGS.

I love cats.

I love wolves, and pandas, and dolphins, and cotton-top tamarins, and honey badgers, and battle unicorns—you call them rhinoceros—and turtles, and . . . you get the picture. I am proudly and without question a member of the Animal Lover contingent.

So, why the nasty little title for this book? Clearly, I am having some fun with the feline king of all How-To screenwriting books. But there's also a point.

Most of you have seen the John Wick films, or at least the first one, which also happens to be the best in my opinion. One of the most successful franchises in recent cinematic history, the John Wick films all start with a single screenplay written by Derek Kolstad—a very good screenplay I might add—which instead of having a cat-saving moment in the first few pages, has the killing of a dog as its inciting incident.

The number of brilliant, successful screenplays that **don't** follow all the cat-saving rules, even going so far as to do the opposite, is too large to list here without this book surpassing Neil Gaiman's *American Gods* in length.

The only number larger is the number of lousy, weak, completely ordinary screenplays that have been written by following the so-called rules.

I want you to move from the latter category to the former, and write brilliant, successful screenplays again and again.

Thus, welcome to *Kill the Dog—The First Book on Screenwriting to Tell You the Truth.*

1

THE ANIMAL IN THE ROOM

I CONSIDERED A few different ways to open this book and decided it was best to begin by addressing the elephant in the room. Or rather, the orange tabby in the room. The one screenwriting book that stands claws and shoulders above all others in terms of sales and recognizability. If you're reading this book, chances are you've read that book. Most everyone who has ever said the word "screenplay" has read that book. I'd wager more people have attempted screenwriting careers because of that book than there are words in the book and all its subsequent offshoots.

How many of those poor souls ever succeeded to any degree? Probably fewer than there are words on the cover of the first book.

While we are not here to bash other books or people, I do need you to be aware of something before you continue.

If you think BLANK CHECK is a better example of good screenwriting and a better script to aspire to than MEMENTO—as claimed multiple times in the Maneki-neko book—then I cannot help you.

This book cannot help you.

I am not sure anyone can help you.

While all art is subjective, there are some things that fall under the category of . . . duh.

One of them is that MEMENTO, whether you like the film or not, is a brilliantly written original screenplay that was nominated for a dozen international screenwriting awards and launched the career of one of the best screenwriters in our business, while BLANK CHECK . . . is not.

If you believe anything other than that, then sure, you may find someone to pay you for writing a screenplay. After all, there have been three different people in history who have won the lottery TWICE.

Most all working professional screenwriters know that the way the Grimalkin book and others like it tell you to write a screenplay is NOT the best way to write one. Or even a good way. In fact, it's a terrible way to write one.

Yes, that's a bold and incendiary statement. But as you continue through the pages you're reading or the audio you're listening to, hopefully, you will begin to get the true picture. Not only will you have a new outlook on what it takes to become a successful working professional screenwriter, but you will be filled with enough inspiration, aspiration, motivation, and all the other "*ations*" to hit levels on your screenwriting journey you never imagined possible.

This is where some of you will say, "*But if that book is wrong WHY is it so popular?*"

I will tell you.

Because it's easy. The book is BRILLIANT (yes, in all caps) in its function of making the reader feel like they don't need to have any talent, knowledge, experience, or even work ethic to write a million-dollar screenplay. The book never even talks about writing. It's all loglines and formulas and math. One of the big lies of the Free the Feline spectacle is it convinces you there is a simple formula to follow for writing great screenplays, and if you follow the steps, you will be buying Malibu beach property with all your WGA residuals in no time.

People love easy. People love to believe they don't need to develop any talent, craft, or skill to succeed at something. A lot of people simply don't want to work hard. Look at the world of influencers and their influence (see what I did there?) on today's youth. In 1980, a poll was conducted of 500 middle schoolers, asking them what they aspired to be when they grow up. Most of them said athlete, firefighter, doctor, astronaut, and the like. The same poll was conducted in 2019 and the most common answer by a large margin was . . . YouTube star. I don't blame the cat book (or any others) for that. My point is these books prey on society's inherent desire for easy.

THE ORIGIN STORY

Kill the Dog was born out of my decades-long frustration with the once cottage, now full-blown industry of screenwriting gurus and all their How-To books and websites.

By the way, I'm going to use the term "guru" a lot. Here's what I mean: a guru is anyone preaching, teaching, selling, or proclaiming they KNOW how best to write a screenplay without ever having done it successfully themselves. And no, selling two co-written scripts to the studio where your father and family friend work does not count.

Ever since the media began reporting the dollar amounts of spec script sales in the 1980s, everyone and their mother (and their mother's landscaper's nephew who lives with a Cracker Barrel waitress in a van behind the Wal-Mart) decided they would simply write a screenplay and become instant millionaires!

Only thing was, 99% of them had no idea what a screenplay was or looked like, let alone how to write one. The only thing that existed at the time was Syd Field's book *Screenplay*, published in 1979.

People started buying that book by the truckloads. This inevitably led to some entrepreneurial souls who saw there were in fact millions of dollars to be made in screenwriting; not by *writing* screenplays, but by telling other people HOW to write them.

There are folks who tried being professional screenwriters but weren't good enough to sustain a career, so they wrote How-To books. What's worse is there are several (very popular) books on screenwriting written by people who never wrote or sold a screenplay in their life!

While *Kill the Dog* may not lead you to the point where you're accepting statues of golden naked people, and while I can't guarantee you a three-picture deal at Warner Brothers, I can absolutely promise you this: you will be a better screenwriter than you were before you read this book. And I believe wholeheartedly that being the very best screenwriter you can possibly be will give you the best chance at success.

It breaks my heart when I hear newer screenwriters who are willing to put in the time and effort, become so depressed because they don't understand why their careers are going nowhere when they're doing EVERYTHING the books and gurus tell them!

And it's not just the books. The internet and subsequently social media have given a voice to the uninformed. You no longer need to have a sand grain amount of knowledge on a subject to speak loudly and voraciously about it.

I have no respect, nor should you, for any book, website, podcast, or social media account doling out screenwriting advice if it's not from a working professional screenwriter.

That may sound rather harsh, but consider this . . .

Let's say you want to learn to play golf as well as you possibly can. You want to become so good that you can do it professionally. Where would you go for instruction? Would you learn from someone who perhaps played golf thirty or forty years ago, but never got that great at it, and now no longer plays the game at all?

Would you learn from someone who is just starting out on their own golf journey, who may know even less than you do, but is happy to tell you how to do it at a high level?

Or . . . would your best decision be to learn from someone who *currently* plays the game at a high level—the level you aspire to—and has done so for a long time; someone who has the experience and pedigree to have an *informed* opinion on how and what it takes to play your best?

There's an old joke about a man who walks into a piano store, sits down at the finest, most expensive piano in the place, and begins to play. And he is absolutely terrible. And he says, "*I don't understand! I've been listening to Mozart my entire life!*"

BULLS IN THE BULLRING

There's an old Spanish proverb that goes, "*To talk of bulls is not the same as to be in the bullring.*" What does that have to do with screenwriting? Or more specifically, all the How-To screenwriting books, websites, and gurus out there?

Gather round, young Jedis . . .

When I began writing this book, I did a search for books on screenwriting. The Google machine provided no less than eleven pages of results. Dozens of How-To books on screenwriting. I stopped counting at 70. All published after Syd's book. Wanna know how many were written by actual working professional screenwriters?

Two. And one of those was a parody.

Now, before you begin yelling, "*What about the rope-hanging tabby! That guy was a professional!*"

Nope, authors like that don't count. Books written by **former** professional screenwriters don't count.

"*Whoa, Guyot, that seems incredibly elitist and unfair.*"

It is not. Here's why:

Most all the How-To books, from the gato emancipation pamphlet to turning Story into Euclidean Geometry, to devolving three-act structure into 22 pointless steps, were written by folks who at one time might have been working professional screenwriters but were out of the business within a very short time. Why? Because they couldn't deliver. They weren't good enough to stay employed.

Here's the thing . . . when someone gets their shot—when they sell a spec script or get hired to write episodes of television—Hollywood comes running. Our industry would much rather go to proven screenwriters who have a track record of being able to deliver than take a chance on some newbie who's never done it. Thus, once you get your shot, you have a massive advantage.

However, just selling a script or writing a couple of episodes of television is no guarantee you will remain employed unless you know how to do it well.

Unless you can deliver again and again.

And selling a couple of scripts or working half a season on one TV show before being fired does not mean you have a clue how to do it well enough to sustain a career.

Let's pause here for those of you thinking, "*Pot, meet kettle!*"

That's fair. Let's unpack that, as the thieves at the airport say.

I have been putting "screenwriter" on my tax returns every year since 1999, including this year, and I will again next year. By the way, Guyot is pronounced "GHEE-oh." Like "Rio." Think GEOSTORM, but with a hard G. *Guyotstorm*. On second thought, don't think about GEOSTORM any more than necessary.

As I type this, I have been a working (meaning employed) professional screenwriter for the past 24 years. The longest I have gone without being paid to write something is ten months.

I have written feature films that have not been made (like many professionals) and ones that have been released (like fewer professionals). I have written and produced well over 200 hours of television. I would estimate close to 90% of all my produced work was written solely by me (as opposed to being co-written).

Most importantly, I am **currently** a working professional screenwriter.

It's a crisp February morning in 2023 as I type these very words you are reading or listening to. At this moment in time, I am under contract with two WGA-signatory companies to write screenplays. I have just completed services on developing a TV series for the international market. My reps are in negotiations on a spec script I wrote that you'll read about later.

These are not gigs from decades past. I am taking time away from my current professional screenwriting gigs to write this book.

What I am not is a *former* professional screenwriter. Or former development executive. Or former reader. Or any of the other monikers the charlatans use to fool you into believing they are qualified to give screenwriting advice.

My membership card in Club WPS—Working Professional Screenwriters—is in good standing, and I even have the cool jacket!

So, why did I write this if I'm not unemployed or desperate for dough? At the risk of sounding overly altruistic, I did it to help.

As I mentioned, the myriad of books out there written by former professionals and never-professionals all claim to have the secret to success. But if they truly knew what it takes, then why weren't they able to sustain success beyond their first couple of gigs?

Despite selling scripts to their father's studio or writing two free-lance episodes of television back when HBO was a little plastic cube on top of your parents' Magnavox called Home Box Office, their careers ended before they really took off. Why? Because they didn't write fresh, original, unique scripts with compelling characters and stories. They wrote flat, paint-by-numbers, formulaic stuff. Even when their specs were made into films which led to pitch meetings and ideas being optioned all over town, they were never paid for another screenplay ever again.

They lost their membership in Club WPS even before they were fitted for the cool jacket.

Even though screenwriters have been disrespected since the days Jack Warner referred to us as nothing but "*Schmucks with Underwoods*," good writing is still the single most desired aspect of the business. Everyone—and I mean EVERYONE—wants a good script. A good writer. When your name is attached to the latest hot script in town, everyone wants to meet you. You get job offers. You get pitch meetings. Whether or not you continue to work as a screenwriter (and optioning pitches is **not** screenwriting) is based on one thing . . . can you deliver again and again?

There's a myriad of ways one can enter Club WPS, but to remain inside the velvet ropes for any significant amount of time, you must write well. Having a "killer logline" and "killer title" might get you meetings, but if you can't write a great script, you'll be writing your own bitter book about how everyone more successful than you sucks.

My goal with this book is to do what none of the other books have done: give you the truth.

Two things are going through some of your minds right now. One is, *'What about all the awful movies that get made? Those scripts suck!"* To that I say, with all due respect, there is simply no way to look at a finished film or television episode and know if the script that started it all was any good. That's another huge problem with all the books. But more on that later. The second thing some of you are thinking or screaming, is, *"It's all nepotism!"*

Yes, it's well-known that nepotism and personal connections hold great power in Hollywood. The industry, as much as it tries to convince itself otherwise, is not a meritocracy. That said, if one does not have the requisite connections or come from a certain gene pool, then one must rely solely on ability.

Most of us arrive in Hollywood with our hopes and dreams packed tightly inside our laptops and don't have fathers or friends who are high-ranking studio execs, or personal relationships with producers and directors. How are we supposed to compete with the Nepo-peeps? We must rely on one thing . . .

Our ability to write quality screenplays again and again.

This book is for the screenwriter who has no family connections, no personal relationships with showrunners, or network execs. In short, folks just like you and me.

So many newer writers I encounter just want to *sell* something. They've written one thing and have no desire to get better at the craft. They just want to sell one thing and hope it leads to dinners with Leo at La Scala and flying private.

It won't.

To quote Scott Frank, one of the best screenwriters working today: *"You have to commit to the writing, not the selling."*

That's the reason behind this book. To give you a chance to sit down with an actual working professional screenwriter and hear the truth. I have always subscribed to Harlan Ellison's quote:

> *You are not entitled to your opinion. You are only entitled to your informed opinion.*

I'm old enough to remember when most folks endorsed this. However, with the advent of social media and the ability to hide behind anonymous (and not-so-anonymous) online handles, the spewing of opinions with no actual knowledge of a subject has become society's norm. Nowhere greater than in the world of screenwriting.

While there have been many books on screenwriting penned by folks who briefly tasted life as a professional screenwriter, there are three or four times as many that have been written by people who have NEVER done it for a living. The best writing these people have accomplished is in crafting their bios to sound like they're some sort of expert.

This book contains my informed opinion on screenwriting. What you will not read here are my opinions on things I have little or no experience with, for example, crab fishing on the Bering Sea, or sitcom writing. I have never worked in the sitcom world, and thus, do not have an informed opinion. Same with crab boats.

That said, if your desire is strictly to write sitcoms, I believe this book can still help you because all great writing, be it an EVERYTHING EVERYWHERE ALL AT ONCE type of feature or a BLACK-ISH sitcom, comes from story and character melded with writing from your soul.

So, let's take the first step toward you becoming a working professional screenwriter.

2

HOLLYWOOD CANNOT EXIST WITHOUT YOU

AFTER THAT RATHER cynical opening, let's get back on the positivity train. I want you to understand—to truly *GET*—how important what you do is to the world of film and television.

Here's a fun fact . . .

Did you know that there are more stars on the Hollywood Walk of Fame for animals than there are for screenwriters? Truth.

What's hilarious about that, and by hilarious, I mean *heartbreakingly sad*, is that the entire Hollywood industry would not exist without screenwriters.

Now, before you say, "*Oh, Guyot, you can say the same thing about directors or actors.*"

No. You can't. Screenwriters are the ONLY people in the global industry of movies and television who create from nothing.

Let me repeat that . . .

Screenwriters are the ONLY people in the entire Hollywood industry who create from nothing.

Every other entity INTERPRETS what the screenwriter creates. The screenwriter sits alone in a room with a blank page, and they create a world of settings and locations, of characters and relationships, of stories filled with dilemma, conflict, emotion, terror, intrigue, joy, you name it, and then everyone else, from directors to post-production, interprets what the screenwriter has created.

Without a writer sitting down and *writing a screenplay,* directors have nothing to direct.

Producers have nothing to produce.

Actors have nothing to say or do.

By the way, I love actors. They are my absolute favorite co-contributors in the creative process. What a good actor can bring to my material is priceless. Actors have made me look way better than I am on multiple occasions.

By interpreting what I created.

Cinematographers, costume designers, sound mixers, music supervisors, gaffers, stunt people, editors, studio marketing folks, and on and on, every single one of them has no job without the screenwriter FIRST creating something from nothing.

The screenwriter is the ONLY entity that creates. All others INTERPRET what the screenwriter creates.

Now, many of these entities can and often do greatly improve the screenplay. I will proudly go on record to say that actors, directors, and editors have elevated my work more often than I can count, but they were all interpreting what I created. They needed a screenplay before they could bring any of their genius to the project.

And just as these interpreters can elevate the material, they can and often do destroy what was once good or even great material.

I, and every other professional screenwriter, would not have a career if it weren't for the lovely artists who come together to make movies and television. The merry band of misfit toys known as a production crew—be it a film or television series—is a nomadic family that comes together for a finite amount of time to tell a story, and that life is one of the most incredible joys I've been blessed to experience when it's gone well. But again, none of it exists, no one in all of Hollywood has a job until the screenwriter types `FADE IN:`

I want you to embrace how critical and needed and valued you are. Do not take this responsibility lightly. Do not just play at screenwriting and expect great results. Don't treat it like some side hustle or a fun thing to do after you've spent the first five hours of your day scrolling social media, and then be disappointed when you never get your Club WPS membership card. If you're serious about a screenwriting career, you must treat it with respect and honor. Otherwise, what's the point? Why half-ass anything, especially something as difficult as this?

As one character in a particularly successful screenplay said, *"Do or do not. There is no try."*

Keep this in mind as you continue through this book and your journey to screenwriting success . . . it cannot happen without you.

3

YOU HAVE ONE JOB

DESPITE ALL THE things you *think* you must remember about screenwriting, all the Do's and Don'ts, all the talk about structure and Voice and Story, there is but one single task you are required to accomplish with your script:

You must elicit an emotional response from the reader.

Let's repeat in bold . . .

YOU MUST ELICIT AN EMOTIONAL RESPONSE FROM THE READER.

Your job is not to tell the story of other people's emotions; your job is to elicit emotions from the reader. Your job is not to write something that will be emotional once it's put on screen. Do that and it will never make it to the screen.

You must elicit an emotional response from THE READER.

You do this by writing. Not by math, not by building some mechanical scaffolding for your story, but by writing. Through language, syntax, characterization, circumstance, surprise, dilemma. There are dozens of ways to elicit an emotional response, and they're all part of the writing. Let's look at one of the most basic and cleanest ways to do this.

Defy expectations.

Why did the chicken cross the road? To get to the other side.

Why does this joke work? Because it defies expectations. We expect something other than the obvious. We expect the unexpected. We expect the reason the chicken crossed the road is going to be shocking or outrageous, something completely out of the ordinary.

But then it surprises us by being completely ordinary. The most obvious Occam's Razor reason for crossing that road.

To get to the other side.

That's why it's funny. That's why it works. It has defied our expectations, and thus, elicited an emotional response.

To defy expectations in your reader does not mean you have to have some huge plot twist or something shocking happen on the page. Sure, those are great ways to do it, but not the only way. You can defy expectations with something that is simply funny, or sad, or scary. It can be something as small as Donny's ashes blowing into The Dude's face in THE BIG LEBOWSKI, or as big as Vader telling Luke he's his father in THE EMPIRE STRIKES BACK (spoiler alert).

Whatever elicits an emotional response. Something that causes our emotion to shift from what it was prior to reading that sentence, scene, or script.

Here are some famous examples of moments that elicited an emotional response by defying expectation (SPOILERS!):

THE GODFATHER—when Michael says he will kill Sollozzo.
PARASITE—when we find Moon-gwang's husband living in the bunker.
MAD MEN—Don Draper is not Don Draper.
CITY OF GOD—Li'l Dice killing the motel people.
CHINATOWN—she's my sister *and* my daughter.
RESERVATION DOGS—the first time the Spirit speaks.
TED LASSO—Ted is good at darts.
SEARCHING FOR BOBBY FISCHER—when Bruce tells Josh all the certificates are fake.
THE BANSHEES OF INISHERIN—too many to list from this amazing script.

You can even defy expectations with tone and setting. Say you need a character to reveal something very bad to another character. Set that scene in the midst of a kid's birthday party with a bouncy house and balloons and happy children running around.

If you need a character to reveal something hilarious set it at a memorial service for a venerable grandmother.

If a reader is cruising through your script and a scene, or character or situation, or even a single line of description is nowhere near what they were expecting, that's good! Even if it's something they hate. This is a writing tightrope we're walking; hating something because the writing is bad versus hating something because it's not what the reader was expecting.

The worst thing a script can do is nothing. I've read dozens and dozens of screenplays that were completely fine from a technical point of view. From, shall we say, a cat-saving, 22-stepping point of view. The formatting, structure, even the story itself was all just fine.

Screenplays aren't supposed to be fine. Capellini is fine. Your screenplay should not be fine.

If it's fine, it's boring. It's a flatline. It does not elicit an emotional response from the reader. Your story, your characters, your words, just sit there on the page. I will go so far as to say a badly written script is better than a "fine" script. A badly written script at least elicits an emotional response. Obviously, not the response the writer wants, but I'd much rather read something so bad I quit after five pages than read 100 pages of something that feels like reading a leaflet on getting your feet scraped.

This is the problem with all the screenplays written by folks who follow the advice of the books and gurus. They hit all the points they're told they must hit; they format the way they're told to format; they describe things the way they are indoctrinated to do so . . .

And they all sound exactly the same. Regardless of whether the story is a huge Sci-Fi action epic or a tale of two sisters working a farm in 1850 Kansas.

THEY ALL SOUND EXACTLY THE SAME.

And that is death when it comes to success as a screenwriter. If your script doesn't sound original, doesn't have a unique Voice, doesn't tell a compelling story with confidence and one's own argot, you are dead.

You have one job . . .

Elicit an emotional response from the reader.

Do your job.

4

WRITE WHAT YOU KNOW

WRITE WHAT YOU KNOW is one of the most debated topics in not just screenwriting but all writing circles. I am firmly in the camp of it being not just good advice, but some of the best writing advice ever given. I will go further and say with complete confidence that people who say Write What You Know is bad advice do not understand what it truly means.

Here's what Write What You Know does NOT mean . . .

Write What You Know does not mean if you're a barista, you should only write stories about making or serving coffee.

It does not mean if you work in a convenience store in Wichita, Kansas, and have never been outside the state you should not write about dragon-riding princesses battling giant laser-eyed creatures across Middle-earth.

It does not mean if you're a transgender BIPOC teenager in Yuma, Arizona, you should not write about old, rich, white men on Wall Street.

It does not mean if you're an altruistic pacifist you can't write about vicious serial killers.

What *Write What You Know* DOES mean is . . .

Write what's inside you.

Write what frightens you.

Write what excites you.

Write what compels you.

Write the things YOU KNOW.

It means put your experiences into your writing. Your *internal* experiences. Your feelings. It doesn't mean write about hiking if you're a hiker. It means write about how hiking makes you *feel* and *why* you love it.

Write What You Know is not external. It is internal.

Have you ever had your heart broken? Remember that pain? Remember those days when you didn't know how or if you could go on? That's what you know. You can take that and put it into your story about dragon-riding princesses in Middle-earth because it's not the actual riding of the dragon that makes those stories memorable; it's the characters and their relationships with each other, and that's where you can elevate your story by writing *what you know.* Bring that pain from your heartbreak into your story of dragon-riding princesses.

Have you been through an abusive upbringing or relationship? You can take those feelings—those feelings you KNOW—and put them into any type of story you wish to write.

Have you ever felt pure joy? Even for a moment? When everything in your world felt perfect? A hug at the right time from the right person. A kiss. A smile. A moment when you felt no weight on your shoulders, no pressure. You KNOW how that feels. Just as you know how it feels when that joy is broken by something or someone and you tumble back down a dark well.

Have you ever been incredibly stressed about an upcoming test because you just found out it's 60% of your final grade, and you didn't study at all? You can infuse that anxiety and regret and fear into any scene that needs it regardless of your story's subject matter.

Think about our transgender BIPOC teen in Yuma. Perhaps they know absolutely nothing about how Wall Street works and the people who populate it. Hello, Google.

What our teen may know is how it feels to be marginalized or ignored. How it feels to be victimized by racism and bigotry. To be underestimated. How it feels to yearn for acceptance and understanding, to be in a crowd yet feel completely alone. Or how it feels to have someone love you for exactly who you are regardless of society's issues.

They can put all that emotion and feeling into their characters and their story of old white men on Wall Street.

How amazing would it be to have a story set in the glamorous, wealthy, cutthroat, white male-dominated world of Wall Street and its power brokers, but was actually about pain and bigotry and overcoming feeling marginalized? About embracing truth and not adhering to society's labels? This amazing underdog character defying the odds (and expectations) to triumph over evil.

I'd be there on opening night!

Write What You Know is not external, it is internal. Sure, if you have experience working inside the world of professional bull riding, you can write a story set there with the accuracy, specificity, and authenticity one cannot get from the Google machine. But that's external. That is not what Write What You Know means.

Write What You Know is not about the technicalities of how you stay on the bull for eight seconds. It's about how you feel when you've been bucked off seventeen times in a row, you've got two broken ribs, you're down to your last dime, your wife is pregnant, and if you don't ride this next bull, you'll lose everything you have. You can KNOW that without ever having been anywhere near a rodeo.

It's about what you're feeling as you climb into that chute; your fear, your pain, your hope, your belief, or lack thereof.

Write What You Know is internal. I cannot repeat that enough.

Consider the following...

Remember that giant Bruckheimer-produced action madness of the late 90s called CON AIR? Well, the screenwriter, Scott Rosenberg, had no personal connection to the plot: an ex-con trapped on a prison transport plane when the prisoners seize control of it. He didn't *know* anything about that. What he did know was how it feels when you're just a guy trying to get home. And that's what he dialed into when he wrote that script.

How about Jordan Peele's 2022 film NOPE? I don't think Jordan knew anything about human-devouring aliens, but what he did know about is Hollywood and the exploitative structure of our industry.

I seriously doubt Shonda Rhimes and Peter Norwalk knew anything about how to get away with murdering people. At least I hope not. But they clearly knew how they felt about trust, loyalty, and revenge, and they infused the writing of HOW TO GET AWAY WITH MURDER with all of that.

If a screenwriter stole cars in their youth, then pens a story about car thieves, or a person who spent a decade as a social worker writes a tale set in the world of social workers, that is not what Write What You Know means. You don't have to have lived a certain type of life to write about it. That's called research.

A screenwriter can research anything. Research is one of the best parts of the gig. But research is external. Say you are researching a story about vets coming back from war with disabilities, and you interview a bunch of them to hear their harrowing stories . . . that's external because those stories are not your story. But you can take all that research and add it to the internal pain you know, add it to the internal feelings you have of loyalty and honor, of feeling ignored or forgotten, and write a helluva script.

When you don't have any feelings or experiences directly connected to your story, then you must look somewhere else inside you.

We call this *finding our way in*. Go back to Rosenberg, Rhimes, and Peele for examples of this.

Write What You Know is about what you know deep down in the core of who you are; what you've experienced, what you feel, what elicits an emotional response in you and why.

So, by all means, WRITE WHAT YOU KNOW.

5

THE WRITER'S VOICE

ALL RIGHT, PUT your phones on Do Not Disturb. If you only pay attention to one chapter in this book, this is it.

Voice is probably the single most important factor in your screenwriting and one of the most misunderstood. Without Voice, you will have little to no chance of ever succeeding as a working professional.

But what is Voice? What does Voice exactly mean? *And why does Guyot keep capitalizing the word?*

Good questions, thanks for asking.

When talking about Voice with a capital V, we are not talking about the voices of the characters, though their voices can be part of Voice. People regularly make the mistake of thinking Quentin Tarantino's Voice is simply his characters' dialogue. But that's inaccurate. If it were true, then O-Ren Ishii would sound just like Vernita Green, and Hans Landa would sound the same as Aldo Raine. They don't.

However, all those characters *sound like Tarantino*. Just like Aaron Sorkin's characters sound like Sorkin. But imagine the Aaron Sorkin version of PULP FICTION.

On second thought, don't do that. Your head might explode.

Shonda Rhimes, Wes Anderson, and Nora Ephron are other screenwriters who come to mind when we think of the screenwriter's Voice coming through their characters' voices.

Taylor Sheridan, Steve Zaillian, and Akela Cooper are screenwriters whose characters' voices aren't nearly as specific as the aforementioned scribes, yet their screenwriter Voices are every bit as strong and unique.

Yes, we are talking about the *screenwriter's Voice*.

Let's have a brief history lesson on Voice when it comes to Hollywood screenwriters . . .

For decades a Hollywood screenwriter's unique Voice held about as much importance to the studios and producers as a writer's favorite color. All the great screenwriters of the Golden Era—Odets, Brackett, Diamond, Krasna, etc.—wrote amazing screenplays but were handcuffed by a system that looked at screenplays simply as variations of stage plays, just blueprints for the final film. Paul Schrader, whose credits include TAXI DRIVER, RAGING BULL, and THE LAST TEMPTATION OF CHRIST, has famously said he believes screenplays are nothing more than blueprints. All due respect to Mr. Schrader, he is wrong. Or at least seven decades out of date.

Screenplays are works of art crafted by artists. Here's my argument for Mr. Schrader:

Before a screenplay can be ANYTHING, before it can be a blueprint for a film or something for directors and actors to interpret, it is a read. Let's repeat that one and put it in all caps.

BEFORE A SCREENPLAY CAN BE ANYTHING, IT IS A *READ*.

Before a script can be an episode of TV, or a feature film, or a seven-minute short; before it can be a project in development or a film that grosses so much at the box office it becomes part of the culture and spawns five sequels; before it can get your name in the Trades, or be a TV series so iconic it leads to Paley Center panels; before it can win Oscars and Golden Globes, or be a film university professors dissect and analyze over and over . . . before it can be any of those things, it is a READ.

And if that read isn't the best it can absolutely be, it will likely never get the chance to be an episode, or film, or project in development, or something so great you need to buy a Justin Wu gown or Caroline Andrew tux for the Oscars.

It is a read before anything else can happen. And if that read isn't great, if it isn't crafted beautifully, if it doesn't elicit an emotional response from the reader, then no director, actor, producer, or studio marketing department will turn it into anything else.

As Alfred Hitchcock said: "*There are three things one needs to make a great film; the script, the script, and the script.*"

As Sidney Lumet told me while standing together staring at Niagara Falls (long story, ask me later), "*I can make a bad film from a good script, but I absolutely cannot make a good film from a bad script.*"

Saying a screenplay is nothing more than a blueprint is like saying a Zaha Hadid design is just a building.

Even QT agrees with me on this; probably the only thing we'll ever agree on.

When you look at scripts from the era of Axelrod and Diamond, they all look and read pretty much the same regardless of who penned them. It's why a lot of movies from the 1930s through the 1960s *sound* very much the same. Yes, there were great writers and not so great writers; writers who wrote character relationships better, writers who exceled at dialogue, or suspense. But the scripts themselves were just variations on stage plays.

Enter William Goldman's BUTCH CASSIDY AND THE SUNDANCE KID.

In 1968 Goldman was a novelist with a pair of small screenwriting credits when he decided to write a movie that he wanted to see and a screenplay he *wanted to read.*

He wrote it in his Voice, his way, without thought to format, "structure," or the way all other screenplays looked and read at the time. He spoke to the reader, he described things we don't see onscreen, he used language and syntax and turns of phrase to make

THE READ as enjoyable as possible. He was not writing just a blueprint for something or someone else.

BUTCH CASSIDY AND THE SUNDANCE KID was unlike any screenplay to ever come before, and it took Hollywood by storm. Every studio wanted it, and eventually Goldman was paid over $400,000 for his script—nearly $4 million in today's bucks.

Goldman's screenplay shifted the paradigm of our industry forever.

Every great script after it, from THE GODFATHER to PULP FICTION to MICHAEL CLAYTON to EVERYTHING EVERYWHERE ALL AT ONCE has been influenced by BUTCH CASSIDY AND THE SUNDANCE KID.

Goldman's script was **ALL** about Voice. Not only was it arguably the best screenplay written to that point, but the movie was a smash. And what happened? The screenwriter's Voice became *the* hot ticket in Hollywood. Screenwriters were finally freed from their "*Schmucks with Underwoods*" existence and became commodities and even forces behind movie deals. Because of Goldman and his script, screenwriters' names were now mentioned in the media, and working professional screenwriters carved out very successful careers because of the unique Voice they bring to the page.

From Jay Presson Allen and Nancy Dowd to Shonda Rhimes and Diablo Cody; from Robert Towne and Shane Black to Charlie Kaufman and Wes Anderson; from Kurt Luedtke and Nora Ephron to Barry Jenkins and Emma Thompson; they all forged award-winning, massively successful careers by writing in their own Voice.

So, what IS Voice exactly? Well, it's *how* a screenwriter writes.

Here's the definition I like:

> *Voice is the distinctive qualities of your own creative personality expressed on the page, including your turn of phrase, syntax, punctuation, character development, and even formatting.*

Yes, formatting is part of Voice.

"*But wait!*" you shout. "*I was taught all screenplays must be formatted to the exact standards taught to us by the OG of gurus, Syd Field, and then retaught by a dozen other folks who didn't know any more than old Syd!*"

Ah, therein lies the rub. Yes, your script must be formatted correctly.**

(Did you see the double asterisks???)

Here's the thing . . . there is formatting, and then there is *formatting*. Remember, this book is about giving you the truth, and the idea that there is only one official way to format your script is . . . a lie. I will cover formatting more deeply in a later chapter I ingeniously call *Formatting*.

For now, I want to talk about formatting as it relates to the screenwriter's Voice. Each screenwriter's unique Voice often includes playing around with formatting to suit their own needs, desires, style, tone, etc.

This does not mean you can send your script off to Hollywood written in crayon on spiral notebook paper and say it's part of your unique writer's Voice. Well, you could, but don't expect that overall deal at Paramount.

It does not mean you can make your sluglines vertical. It does not mean you can put all your character names in 18pt Wingdings while the rest of your script is written in 8pt Baskerville Old Face.

You *could* do all this, but unless your screenplay is the greatest collection of words since CITIZEN KANE, chances are you will be kicked out of show business and have to go work at your cousin's storage facility in Palmdale. Nobody wants to work there. Not even your cousin.

What it does mean is you can *play* with formatting in the way Barry Jenkins, the Gilroy brothers, Erin Cressida Wilson, and many others do.

But . . . none of these writers do it for the sake of doing it. Every time there's a change in what folks perceive as the standard traditional formatting, there must be a good reason behind it.

Good reasons to play with formatting:

- Creating more emotional impact
- Creating a specific tone
- A desire for the reader to know a particular word/section/etc. means something special

Bad reasons to play with formatting:

- Because it will look different or *cool*
- Because the writer is a contrarian
- Any reason not listed under Good

Here are a couple of examples of what I mean by playing with formatting. The first is from the opening page of Eric Red's NEAR DARK, still one of the best vampires flicks ever.

```
"NEAR DARK"

FADE IN:

A MOSQUITO alights on a human arm.
The stinger injects in the warm flesh.
The insectile body becomes full and red as it sucks
the blood.
The fist of the arm clenches.
The forearm muscles tighten.
Trapping the stinger.
The mosquito struggles to pull its needlelike
appendage free.
The tendons of the arm hold it firm.
Forcing blood into it.
The insect struggles.
Blood engorges it, swelling its body.
It swells.
Swells.
POPS in a SPRITZ of blood.
```

```
                    CALEB
          Dumb suck.

INT. FLATBED - FORD PICKUP - DUSK

CALEB COLTON is stretched out on the beat up, broke
down '64 Ford Pickup.
Cowboy boots crossed on the transom.
Hat dipped low over his face.
He is a strapping young farmboy of 18.
Long, dusty, shoulder length hair.
An all-American, milkbread, midwestern farm kid.
Bored off his ass.
He yawns and swings off the back of the truck.

EXT. OKLAHOMA FLATLANDS - DUSK

The pickup is a funnel of dust on the thin strip of
road.
The wide open, bleak emptiness of the fields as far
as the eye can see.
An awesome country sunset spreading out across
the sprawling, barren landscape in fingers of red
shadows.
```

Red gave every sentence in the script its own individual line. And he does this throughout the entire script.

This would make any guru's head explode. But it works. It breaks the non-existent rules by doing something no one would think of doing. Why did Eric Red write it this way? You'd have to ask him. I would wager that it goes to the tone of the read.

Despite the fact Red was writing this for (and eventually with) Kathryn Bigelow to direct, he knew that before it could ever be a movie in production, the screenplay was a read. By putting each sentence on its own line, Red gives the read a tone and feel that matches almost perfectly with the Neo-vampire Noir-Western vibe of the story.

For a more contemporary example, let's look at Dan Gilroy's Oscar-nominated screenplay NIGHTCRAWLER.

```
The MAN sees LOU listening, slams the door shut and
CUT TO A LOS ANGELES TV STATION in the high numbers
on Sunset ... neon sign flickering against the
night ...
```

KWLA-TV
Television Center

```
INSIDE THE STATION

LOU enters the NEWSROOM where a night shift skeleton
CREW is cobbling together the morning broadcast ...

LOU moving unnoticed through the open room ... eyes
taking in everything ... HALF-DOZEN WRITERS typing
copy in cubicles ...
```

Oh, no! Someone call Tony Gilroy and tell him his brother is about to get kicked out of Show Business! The gurus say you CAN'T have fonts any bigger than 12pt in your screenplay!

Well, guess what? This is page 14, and it's the *third* time he's dropped in some crazy-ass font. Oh, the humanity!!

If this script went to any of the "experts" charging money on the internet to give notes on screenwriting, what's the first thing they'd say?

DON'T PUT BIG FONTS IN YOUR SCRIPT!

And they will tell you it will make you look like an amateur. That no working professional screenwriter would ever do this.

Except for the guy who was nominated for an Oscar.

Bulls in the bullring.

While formatting is certainly one aspect of the screenwriter's Voice, it is showcased more often in the way the script is *written*.

I'm amazed how few of the How-To books, especially the pusa one, EVER mention WRITING. They talk about everything but writing.

Writing is language. The language of your script. The gurus love to tell you HOW to write sluglines and dialogue, and what page to put what incident on, and they really love telling you what *not* to do. But they never talk about the *writing*. Why?

Because they don't know.

Remember, it's not called screenstructure, or screenstory, or screenidea . . . it's screenWRITING. And the better written your script is, the better your chances of success.

Language is the turn of phrase, syntax, punctuation, the very sentences on the page. This is where Voice truly shines.

I want to show you what I believe are two of the best examples of Voice in the history of screenwriting. I am not claiming either of these are the two best scripts ever written, though, you can certainly make an argument for either one, I am simply sharing with you my favorite expressions of Voice.

The first takes us back to Goldman's industry-changing BUTCH CASSIDY AND THE SUNDANCE KID. Goldman's Voice jumps out at us even before the story begins when, on the first page *before* the screenplay begins, it reads:

```
Not that it matters, but what follows is true.
```

Seems innocuous enough, right? Only it had never been done before. Anything before it (and most after) was some version of "*Based on a true story.*" But Goldman brought his Voice into it.

The truly spectacular example of Goldman's argot comes on page 26—and this scene is legendary in screenwriting circles—when Butch and Harvey Logan are about to engage in a knife fight to see who will be in charge of the Hole-In-The-Wall gang . . .

```
Butch moving through the gang toward Logan. He is
unarmed and a knife is offered him by one of the
gang.

                    BUTCH
          Not yet.
              (moving up to Logan now)
          Not til Harvey and me get all the rules
          straight.

                    LOGAN
          Rules? In a knife fight? No rules!

As he finishes speaking, Butch delivers the most
aesthetically exquisite kick in the balls in the
history of the modern American cinema.
```

I could read that another hundred times and still love every single syllable.

Think that's a blueprint, Schrady? That line exists for no other reason than THE READ.

Speaking of Goldman's Voice, and specifically this screenplay, he did so many things which had never been done, that even working professional screenwriters have since attempted to find their own Voice by channeling Goldman. Just like when we're starting out and writing fanfic of our favorite screenwriters. Most professionals do their own versions of Goldman's Voice, but some (I'm looking at you, William Monahan) just flat rip off old Bill. What a massive compliment.

The second example is from what I believe to be the best screenplay written in the last thirty or forty years.

MICHAEL CLAYTON by Tony Gilroy.

This example of Gilroy's Voice defies every guru- and professor-instituted doctrine ever uttered. The scene comes just 15 pages into the script. However, it's a flashforward, and we will come to realize the scene actually takes place on page 114, just before the end of the film.

But this first scene, barely 15 minutes into the finished film, is written in such an elegant, beautiful, and compelling way that the reader is immediately drawn deeply into this character and his psyche. This connection makes it impossible not to feel complete empathy for Clayton despite knowing almost nothing about the character at this point.

```
EXT. THE FIELD - DAWN

Michael getting out of the car. Standing there.

THREE HORSES poised at the crest of the pasture.
Hanging there in the fog like ghosts.

MICHAEL jumping the fence. Walking slowly into the
field. Behind him, the MERCEDES with the engine
running.

THE HORSES aware of him now, watching him come.

MICHAEL'S FACE as he walks. And later on we'll
understand all the forces roiling inside him, but for
the moment the simplest thing to say is that this is
a man who needs more than anything to see one pure,
natural thing, and by some miracle he has found his
way to this place. The wet grass and cold air and no
coat - none of it makes any difference to him right
now - he's a pilgrim stumbling into the cathedral.

And he stops. Just standing there. Empty. Open. Lost.

Nothing but the field and the fog and the woods
beyond.

The HORSES staring at him.

MICHAEL staring back.
```

This, dear readers, is VOICE.

Absolutely pure, unique, authentic writing. I've seen the film many times. I've read various drafts of the script over a dozen times, and I am still moved emotionally every time I read this scene. And THAT is the job of the screenwriter.

Not to create a blueprint for others, not to write something that fits within certain rules and formulas, not to create a "business plan," or any of the other lies.

To elicit an emotional response in the reader.

And here's the cherry on this screenwriting sundae: Gilroy (like Goldman) wrote this solely for the read.

Gilroy ignores guruspeak like: "*gotta have lots of white on the page*" and "*gotta keep your action lines to four max!*" and "*never describe anything we can't see on screen!*"

Gilroy is WRITING the story. He is giving zero thought to what the uninformed say one should or should not do when screenwriting. He is not thinking about anything other than telling a story as evocatively as he can. Writing his story his way in his Voice. And because of that, it is absolutely brilliant.

I believe you can learn more about screenwriting from reading this one script than by reading all the How-To books combined.

Every one of us has our own singular Voice when it comes to screenwriting. Just as I cannot write a script in the Voice of Tony Gilroy, he cannot write a script in my Voice. Nor would he want to. But he cannot write a script in Shonda's Voice. She cannot write in Shane Black's Voice. They all write in their own Voice.

Some of you are probably thinking, "*What about when you're on a television show and have to write in the showrunner's Voice?*"

I have good news: you don't have to worry about that.

It's not so much a lie as a misconception. You don't ever write in the showrunner's Voice. You write the showrunner's characters and stories in the show's voice. I do a deeper dive on this in a few pages.

Let's get back to Voice.

Do not be afraid of it. Despite what all the gurus say you are not allowed to do, embrace your own Voice. Tell your story your way. Don't aspire to write like thousands of others have who listened to the same junk and followed the same rules from the same books—and had little or no success.

I was going to create another chapter where I talk about telling a story vs. reporting a story. Then I realized that discussion is really part of Voice.

TELLING A STORY vs REPORTING A STORY

What do I mean by telling vs. reporting? Well, you've heard the old *Show, don't tell* adage, right? What that means is behavior is more interesting than backstory.

Similarly, when a story is simply reported in a screenplay, all emotion is removed. It's why folks giving us the news on television are called reporters and not storytellers. I'm talking about the actual news, not opinion shows masquerading as news.

When it comes to screenwriting, the reporting of your story is Xanax for the reader. There's no faster way to put them to sleep. I remember reading a spec pilot from a writer we were considering hiring that had one of the most original ideas I'd come across in a long time. However, the writing was so bland, so colorless, so absent of Voice, that it wrecked the potential of their story.

And reporting your story is exactly what all the books and gurus and social media experts advise you to do. They talk about everything EXCEPT writing. Language, syntax, etc. All the things that make up your Voice.

Here's an example of what it looks like when a screenwriter simply reports a story:

```
INT. RESTAURANT - NIGHT

Montgomery eats in a fancy restaurant that is closed to
the public. Chaz sits across from him watching him eat.

                    MONTGOMERY
          I'm not hearing good things.

                    CHAZ
          We are moments away.

                    MONTGOMERY
          Moments away from success? Disaster?
          Orgasm?
```

Seems fine, right? What's wrong with that? It reads like thousands of other screenplays. That's the problem. There's no Voice. No storytelling. Just a report.

Now, compare the above reporting the story with *telling the story*:

```
INT. MELISSE RISTORANTE - LOS ANGELES - NIGHT

Montgomery has this Michelin-starred eatery all to
himself.

He's on the 4th of a 7-course tasting meal... Sonoma
lamb crusted in coffee.

Chaz sits across from him watching this spectacle.

                    MONTGOMERY
          I'm not hearing good things.

                    CHAZ
          We are moments away.

Montgomery savors a bite. Gotta be the coffee. Chaz
watches, remembering the chili dog he had for dinner.

Montgomery sips from his glass of 2016 Paul Hobbs
Beckstoffer To Kalon Cab.

                    MONTGOMERY
          Moments away from success? Disaster?
          Orgasm?
```

Which version is more evocative? Which version draws you in more as the reader? Which version can you visualize better? Which elicits an emotional response? The second version would be condemned by gurus who claim you must never write anything you can't see on screen like Chaz thinking about the chili dog. The gurus are wrong. Goldman, Gilroy and all the other Club WPS members prove it.

Being specific is another key component of Voice. Don't just say "eats dinner" when you can describe what's being eaten. If you're thinking the director or producer or prop department might have issues with your specificity, guess what? That means someone bought your script and it's being made! And there's a good chance the reason it was purchased is THE READ elicited an emotional response.

Do you see what I'm talking about here?

Let's go back to Gilroy's scene of Michael Clayton and the horses.

Imagine if you will, this very same scene, but instead of telling us a story the way Gilroy did, describing internal thoughts and painting a beautiful emotional image, it was written the way the books and gurus would have you write it: simply reporting the story.

```
EXT. FIELD - DAWN

Michael gets out of the car and stands in a foggy
field.

He sees some horses. He walks toward them.

He stares at them, thinking.
```

Did I say Xanax? Make that Dilaudid.

It's the exact same scene, isn't it? However, Gilroy's version is telling us the story in the moment, the guru version is simply reporting what we see onscreen.

Which version do you think is better? Which version connects us to the character? Which version elicits an emotional response from the reader?

So many self-proclaimed experts tell newer screenwriters to never put anything in your screenplay you can't see. No internal thoughts, no excessive descriptions, only write exactly what the viewer can see onscreen. If that's true, then here's just a partial list of the screenwriters who have been doing it wrong.

- William Goldman
- Tony and Dan Gilroy
- Erin Cressida Wilson
- Shonda Rhimes
- QT
- Billy Ray
- Paul Thomas Anderson
- John Rogers
- John August
- John Ridley
- Shane Black
- Aaron Sorkin
- Akela Cooper
- Nora Ephron
- Beck & Woods
- Barry Jenkins
- Phoebe Waller-Bridge
- The Coen Brothers
- Kwan & Scheinert
- Steve Zaillian
- Simon Kinberg
- Michaela Coel
- Craig Mazin
- Emma Thompson
- Richard Wenk
- Damien Chazelle
- David Mamet
- Paul Haggis

Yeah, they'll never make it as screenwriters. Better to follow the advice of folks who lost their Club WPS cards or never had one to begin with.

We are *storytellers*. Not story reporters.

Ah, but I will gladly admit that part of the truth of what it takes to be a working professional screenwriter is there is no single way to succeed. Someone could do the opposite of everything I say in this book and succeed. Not likely, but possible. What I am doing is giving you the best way to increase your chances of success. There are ways to do things that will increase your chances just as there are ways to do things that will greatly hurt your chances.

The odds of you writing a fresh, entertaining, original script in your own Voice by doing exactly what all the gurus tell you to do and not do are . . . bad. Like winning the lottery twice bad. But hey, I'm sure it's happened.

The odds of succeeding by writing a fresh, entertaining, original script in your own Voice, by trusting yourself, by writing and writing, and rewriting and rewriting, ignoring all the white noise from those who can't do it, are much, much better than the lottery ticket approach.

Think of it this way . . . you want to make one million dollars. You can play the lottery every week hoping you hit. Or you can work very hard at something, save and invest your money well.

Both scenarios could absolutely lead to you having a million dollars. Which one gives you a better chance? The charlatans want to convince you that playing the lottery is the only way. I'm telling you being smart and working hard is another way.

The choice is yours.

Let's talk about Rian Johnson.

Rian Johnson is a fantastic writer-director. Rian Johnson also happens to love McKee's *Story*—a How-To book I and hundreds of other working professionals don't love. We believe the book makes storytelling way more complex than it needs to be. Not to mention it was written by a dude who tried desperately to be a professional screenwriter but failed. But Johnson's brain is wired in a much more engineering way than an imaginative way. So, engineering his story first and believing (from a structural standpoint) the tail wags the dog works for him.

Johnson is a rare individual blessed with an engineer's brain and an artist's soul. Johnson combines the two to create wonderful screenplays in his own unique Voice. But before you decide to emulate Rian Johnson you must first take a deep and honest look at yourself and decide if his way is the best way for you. Just because Johnson is phenomenally successful in doing it his way does not guarantee you will see any success by copying his process. And here's the interesting thing . . . anytime I've heard Johnson speak about screenwriting, he talks about all this engineering he does up top, then invariably says something along the lines of, "*But when I start writing, all that stuff kind of goes out the window.*" That said, if you think you have Johnson-level talent, knock yourself out.

I see this type of decision making a lot with QT disciples. The aspiring professional screenwriters who believe Tarantino walks on creative water believe doing it the way he does it will lead them to the promised land of Tarantinoian emperorship.

It won't. And there are *thousands* of failed screenwriters since October 14th, 1994 to attest to this truth. There is only one QT. Hollywood already tried copying him. Remember the first few years after PULP FICTION when the theaters were filled with crappy QT knock-offs? How many of those writers ever worked again?

The reason Rian Johnson is a great screenwriter is not because he got anything amazing from the McKee book, just as the reason Craig Mazin is great is not that he renounces books like that. They are great because they write IN THEIR OWN VOICE.

To repeat: Voice is the single, most critical aspect of your screenwriting and will give you your greatest chance of success.

Go read a QT script. Or Phoebe Waller-Bridge, or Charlie Kaufman. Their tremendous success is due to their Voice, not to their adherence to nonexistent rules.

Voice is the best way to make your script stand out from the rest; to not sound like the dozen other scripts an agent, producer, or executive reads that weekend. Nobody on the planet has your Voice. Only you do. Trust it.

It is time to stop believing the lie that you must write a screenplay exactly as all other screenplays are written. What makes a great screenplay is the *writing*. Not the visuals or logline or title or inciting incidents or page count or formatting, but *the written execution of the story*. And the most critical part of executing your screenplay is Voice. If the Voice isn't there, it doesn't matter how good anything else might be, you're done.

Okay, how many of you are thinking, "*Well, those names are all A-List screenwriters, so they can write however they want. But when you're starting out you have to follow the rules!*"

Be honest. You were thinking that, right? Hey, I get it. But allow me to blow that argument off the face of the planet once and for all. And please, I give you full permission to use what I'm about to tell you the next time someone makes the absurd *A-Listers can do what they want* statement.

The idea that QT, Sorkin, Shonda, the Gilroys, the Coens, and all the others can write the way they want to is because they are A-Listers . . . **IF** that were true . . . then that means when they were starting out, they wrote differently than they do now. That they all wrote the same way the gurus and books tell you to write, but then once they became A-Listers, they CHANGED how they write their screenplays.

Really? That's the story you're going with? That somewhere there are scripts penned by all the A-Listers written in some by-the-numbers, Voiceless, unoriginal way? Scripts with none of their unique language or phrasing or formatting?

Can someone please send me one? I'd love to read it.

The idea that A-list screenwriters changed the way they write once they became A-Listers is so ludicrous and so incredibly ignorant I can barely contain myself.

THE REASON THEY BECAME A-LISTERS IS BECAUSE THEY HAVE ALWAYS WRITTEN IN THEIR OWN VOICE!

Sheesh.

"Okay, Guyot, so how do I find my Voice???"

Great question. The answer, not so great.

The answer, the truth, is . . . you find your Voice by writing.

And writing. And writing. And writing.

But NOT by writing the way the books tell you to write. You find it by writing YOUR way. That's how you discover your Voice. How can you ever expect to find your Voice if you're always writing screenplays in the same generic way the books tell you to?

While you are writing and rewriting your way without thought to any of the so-called rules, you will find your Voice. I promise you.

Here's more truth . . . in the beginning none of us have our own Voice. How could we? We haven't written enough. What makes it even harder to find your Voice in today's screenwriting realm is the white noise from the gurus and websites and social media that causes us to question ourselves. White noise is a powerful villain. Marvel should create an evil character named White Noise whose superpower is whenever they're around you can't hear yourself think. I was blessed to not have any social media or YouTube when I started out. If I had, I promise you I wouldn't be writing this book right now. I'd be asking if you want fries with your burger.

Back then I LOVED Scott Rosenberg's scripts. He was far and away my favorite screenwriter. So, all my early stuff is bad Scott Rosenberg fanfiction. I didn't have my own Voice, but I knew the type of writing I loved, and so I emulated it. I was not consciously copying Rosenberg, I was just trying to write as well as I could, and his stuff was the best I was reading at the time. So, I tried to write my scripts like his scripts.

I wrote all the time. I worked as a Stand-in in my younger years and spent hours upon hours on movie sets with nothing to do. I just wrote. And wrote. I read and read. Not just screenplays, but books. Short stories. Poetry. I fed my writer's soul. And something began to happen.

The more I wrote, the less faux Rosenberg my stuff became and the more Guyot it started to be. I began to find my own Voice. There really is no other way to find it.

I was not aware I was finding my Voice. At the time, I had no idea what Voice was. Nobody talked about it, nobody explained it.

I was a longtime fan of HK Cinema by the time QT hit the scene, so I was one of the few not overly impressed with this new kid in town because I was familiar with the OGs whom he was, uh, "inspired by." That said, QT's Voice is absolutely one of the strongest and most unique in the industry, and it's why he's able to create work that seems so much more original than it is.

Once I found my Voice my writing leveled up, and it did not take long for me to find work. Rob Thomas (the writer, not the singer) gave me my very first paid gig writing a freelance episode for a show called SNOOPS. Before that episode even aired, JJ Abrams hired me to join the staff of FELICITY. Both jobs came after each showrunner had read a spec NYPD BLUE of mine. It was during the interview for FELICITY when I first heard the term Voice.

JJ mentioned my Voice in the NYPD BLUE script, saying how

impressed he was I managed to write in my own Voice yet still make the script sound like it was an actual episode of the show.

I just nodded and said thanks, having no clue what he was talking about.

That story brings me to the inevitable question some of you will ask:

> *How do you write an episode of someone else's TV show in your Voice? Don't you have to be able to write in the showrunner's Voice?*

Ah, one of the more common myths in Hollywood: if you want to be a television writer you have to write in the showrunner's Voice.

Not true.

What you must be able to do is write well, and part of writing well is being able to write a show in the voice of the show—not the showrunner.

The showrunner and/or the number-two on staff will take care of rewriting your script to sound the way they want it to. All you need to do is write well. Understand how to tell a good story, how to create good characters, and how to do all that screenwriter stuff in your own Voice.

Here's the thing . . . it's impossible for you to write in the Voice of a showrunner. We all have our own unique writer's Voice. Sure, it's possible to copy someone (think back to my derivative Rosenberg fan-fiction), but you will never be able to write in *their* Voice.

Whether you are writing on the staff of someone else's show, or you're writing a pilot someone has paid you a fortune to write with five non-writing EPs looking over your shoulder, regardless of the boxes you are forced to color inside, you can still put yourself into the work. Let me rephrase that—you **must** put yourself into the work. And you do that with Voice.

The truth is even on the shows where you hear horror stories of showrunners who want their writers to be nothing more than little robots of dictation, you will fail miserably if you try to alter your writing to sound like theirs.

Showrunners hire writers with great Voices. Even notorious showrunners like Matt Weiner, David E. Kelley, Sorkin, etc. The reason those great writers hire you is not because they think you write like them, it's because of your own Voice. They read something of yours and like it enough to meet you and hire you. They want you to write in your own Voice. It doesn't matter if it's light years from their Voice because they're going to rewrite you anyway. I can't emphasize this enough. You are not hired to write television because a showrunner thinks you can copy them. You are hired because they think you're a good writer.

When I wrote for a David E. Kelley show, I turned in my first script and the Co-Executive Producer (Hart Hanson) called me into his office saying he had great news. "*Guess what? David loved your script! He only rewrote ninety percent of it!*" Hart wasn't being funny or sarcastic, he was serious. The fact DEK left 10% of my own writing in the script was apparently a huge victory and tremendous confirmation of my ability to do this screenwriting thing.

I guarantee you no quality showrunner will ever hire a writer whose work is Voiceless and generic. They want WRITERS. Writers who have a Voice. If you get on their shows and then try to write *like* them, they won't rewrite you, they'll fire you.

I was a Co-Executive Producer on a show where there was a writer in their first year of staffing. I had read their original pilot which got them the meeting and subsequent hire, and their Voice was great. However, every script they turned in for the show was a disaster. It was bland and flat and generic. This person was trying so hard to write and sound like the showrunner, they ended up just writing badly.

This is the same thinking that makes the final product of so many potentially good or great films so bad. The company starts out with a great script everyone is excited about. It's fresh and original, has a Voice, elicits emotion. Then the development process begins, and the money people in their infinite wisdom (and complete paranoia) begin to water it down, thinking maybe the story is too specific or has too narrow a POV. So, they change it in an attempt to make it appeal to everyone, and in doing so they make it appeal to no one. They rob it of its POV.

Of its Voice.

As a screenwriter, do not write like a paranoid studio executive.

If you look at the episodes I wrote for, say, FELICITY back in the day, alongside episodes I wrote of NCIS: NEW ORLEANS twenty years later—I'm talking about the first drafts prior to being rewritten by someone else—you will see/feel/hear my Voice. There's an evolution in my writing because I was getting better as the years went on, but my Voice is the same. It's the Voice you're reading right now. I was never consciously trying to impart my Voice into my work, rather I was simply writing the things I wanted to read. Voice only happens when you don't try to write in your Voice. It happens when you trust yourself and write for yourself, as opposed to trying to write like others before you as the gurus preach.

One of the great rewards of writing for Barbara Hall (JUDGING AMY) and John Rogers (LEVERAGE, THE LIBRARIANS) is both showrunners were so secure with themselves that they encouraged their writing staff's own Voices to come out in the finished episodes. They didn't want anyone trying to be anything other than who they were. Hall and Rogers are intelligent enough to understand one does not need to imitate a showrunner on the page or make every script sound identical to have a television series with a consistent voice. When you watched an episode of JUDGING AMY you could always tell if it was a Barbara Hall episode or one written by Barry O'Brien, or Lyla Oliver. Same on Rogers's shows; you knew when an episode had been penned by Geoff Thorne, Amy Berg, Becky Kirsch, etc. As showrunners, they might tweak something here or there to make sure it was on point with the characters they created, but the writer's individual Voice was celebrated while still maintaining the voice of the show. Yes, it's possible.

I never worked on a Vince Gilligan series, but I would guess he is the same way. Because I could always tell when I was watching an episode written by him, or by George Mastras or Gennifer Hutchinson. Yet, every episode WAS the show.

So, please get this myth out of your head that television writers must alter who they are or how they write in order to imitate a showrunner.

Even when I worked on shows where the showrunners were less secure than Hall and Rogers, did I change the way I write? Try to alter my Voice?

No.

If I did anything different, I might tweak the way I *express* things on the page. To perhaps make the writing feel a little less like me the individual and a little more like the dictation machine the showrunner wanted. This is NOT trying to write in the Voice of the showrunner. Try that, and you'll be checking ZipRecruiter in no time.

I've irritated you again, haven't I? This isn't why one buys a book on screenwriting, eh?

"Come on, Guyot, where's the hack? The formula? I need one of those charts or graphs or circle thingys!"

Sorry, folks. Consult the other books for that. This one is for those of you who want to become successful working professionals.

6

LET'S TALK ABOUT THE F WORD

FORMATTING.

If there's one thing the gurus love to preach about, it's formatting. They tell you it is an absolute moral imperative for you to format your script "properly." Properly being a euphemism for *It must be done this exact singular way without the slightest deviation, otherwise you will never be allowed inside the gates of Hollywood!*

Let me drop some truth on you regarding formatting.

First, if you want to learn proper formatting, you do not need to spend money on books. Just read produced screenplays. The internet is filled with them. Reading two or three scripts will teach you everything you need to know about formatting. For free.

Unlike most other aspects of screenwriting, formatting does have its "rules," but there are fewer of them than you've been told, and they aren't what you think they are.

I am assuming the fact you're reading this book means you have seen a professional screenplay at some point. Not something your favorite barista wrote, but an actual produced screenplay written by a professional screenwriter. One with all those INT.s and EXT.s, and (V.O.)s and whatnot. While there is a general form to a screenplay's format, there are very few *rules*. Let's discuss the most familiar ones:

SLUGLINES

Sluglines are those lines that usually start with INT. or EXT. indicating the following scene is either an interior or exterior. These exist solely for the production of the project; for the producers and crew to know if the shoot will be inside or outside. It's used for spec scripts simply because it's tradition. Classic. Like Adidas Stan Smiths. But it is *not a rule.*

WHAT???

Before you have an embolism, let me explain.

Here's an example of the traditional (classic) slugline for a scene that takes place inside a restaurant's kitchen during the day:

```
INT. RESTAURANT - KITCHEN - DAY
```

While this example is the classic slugline, it is not a rule. Just look at scripts by William Goldman, Greta Gerwig, Barry Jenkins, or everyone's favorite, QT, and many others.

So long as the reader understands where the scene is happening, you are good to go. For our same restaurant kitchen scene, here are some variations on the classic slug that don't follow the traditional example yet are absolutely acceptable.

```
INT. RESTAURANT/KITCHEN/DAY
```

```
INT. RESTAURANT. KITCHEN. DAY
```

```
INT. RESTAURANT - KITCHEN
```

```
INT. KITCHEN INSIDE RESTAURANT
```

```
RESTAURANT KITCHEN
```

```
KITCHEN
```

```
INSIDE RESTAURANT KITCHEN
```

```
INSIDE KITCHEN BACK OF RESTAURANT
```

Or any variation of the above. ALL of these are acceptable.

You can underline your sluglines or not. You can **bold** or *italicize*. Feel free to add `DAY` or `NIGHT` or `MORNING`, or don't. You can use a dash (—), or a slash (/), or a period. You can leave out the INTs and EXTs if you like—it won't affect the read at all. If your script sells and goes into development, the INTs and EXTs will get added.

You have my word; it does not matter. Do it your way.

Time for another pause because I can hear some of you already yelling about those contests you enter and websites you pay for notes and feedback: "*If it's not formatted in the right way, they will . . .*"

I'm gonna stop you right there. Here's the thing . . . all those contests are a waste of time (more on that in a later chapter), and as to the sites offering judgment and critique on your work for a price . . . if they were people who actually knew anything about professional screenwriting, they would know it doesn't matter. Any entity that would consider your work lower quality due to using a less common slugline or playing with formatting the way professionals do, is an entity you should run from. They cannot and will not help your career. They will only hurt it. The notes you get from folks who are not working professional screenwriters can derail your career faster than Michael Bay kicks over a monitor. I've seen it happen, both the derailing and the kicking. So, stop giving money to those entities.

Okay, back to formatting.

I will change up my formatting on each script I write depending on how I want the read to feel. There is a rhythm to good writing. I believe the read of a screenplay should feel like music. It's all about rhythm and tone. The way your script is formatted will affect that rhythm and tone.

I wrote a big, glossy heist feature and the music of that script was most definitely jazz. So, I wrote it in a language that felt like jazz, including how I formatted it.

I underlined and bolded my sluglines, and once I established if it was Day, Night, etc., I did not continue to add the extra word to every subsequent slugline that took place during that same time. I used one space between sentences as opposed to two—another so-called rule that is not a rule at all. One space or two DOES NOT MATTER. 100% up to the writer.

How did this tweaking of format make my script feel like jazz? I have no clue. It just felt that way to me as the writer. And trusting your writer gut is always a good bet.

When I had to adapt a dark Korean action film for a studio recently, I wanted a completely different tone. The music of the read was darker, more somber, bleak. I wrote in much shorter, staccato sentences. I used a lot of ellipses. I double-spaced between sentences. Why? Because the story was stark and lonely. I wanted a feeling of sparseness for the read. I still underlined my sluglines but did not bold them.

The heist script was fun and light, so I made sure the read was as well. With the action story, I wanted the tone and rhythm of the read much more Mowg than Chico Hamilton.

In 2019 I wrote a comedy pilot which sold to a network on a Thursday, and then unsold the following Monday (because the head of the network split with her husband over the weekend). It contained sluglines with no bold or underline, one space after sentences, and TWO dashes between the location and the time of day. Why? Who knows? I just did it in the moment and liked the way it looked and felt. I wasn't trying to write to anyone else's idea of what's correct or incorrect.

Instead of giving a slugline to every new location I often just put it in CAPS. The rhythm and tone of that piece was '80s music; Flesh for Lulu, Love and Rockets, Echo & The Bunnymen, and that's how I tried to write it.

Let's pause here to go over the very few "rules" there are in formatting. While I have seen these broken a time or two, it usually doesn't help the read, and anything that doesn't help the read . . . hurts.

PARENTHETICALS

Parentheticals are the little helpers you see in a character's dialogue. They go under the character's name and above their first line but can also be inserted above any line of dialogue. Example:

```
                    LARRY
                (distracted)
          Sure, I can do that.
```

Or . . .

```
                    LARRY
          Sure, I can do that.
              (looks up)
          What'd you say?
```

Parentheticals exist when the writer feels a need to convey a certain, specific behavior or tone during dialogue. Parentheticals can become crutches very easily, so please use them sparingly. The most egregious use of parentheticals I see with newer writers is adverbs. Bad adverbs. The type with -LY on the end. That's a flashing red sign the writer isn't confident in their own work.

If you find yourself adding a lot of parentheticals in your dialogue like "sadly," "jealously," or "angrily," it's a good chance one or more of the following is happening:

- You have no confidence your writing is conveying the proper emotion; you're afraid the reader won't "get it."
- You have not developed your characters enough so that they have a point of view.
- You have not given your characters their own unique voices. See our chapter on dialogue for more on this.

Parentheticals must also always be relevant to the character who is speaking. Meaning, never use a parenthetical to describe something that is not directly related to the dialogue of the character who is speaking. Here is an example of the *incorrect* use of a parenthetical:

```
                    LARRY
          You don't remember that?
              (a car pulls up outside)
          It was the night we had lasagna.
```

The car pulling up needs its own action line, otherwise what you are conveying to your reader is that Larry's line about the lasagna is said *because* the car pulls up which makes no sense.

If you want Larry's line to be a reaction to the car, then you write it like this:

```
                    LARRY
          You don't remember?
              (a car pulls up outside)
          I hope that's the lasagna.
```

The placement of the parenthetical is one of the very few formatting "rules" I do believe should be adhered to in every script. The worst mistake is when the writer puts parentheticals on the same line as the dialogue.

```
                    LARRY
          You don't remember? (a car pulls up
          outside) I hope that's the lasagna.
```

Never do this. Why? Because it breaks the flow of the read. The reader's brain must stop and decipher that those words are not dialogue, but rather an action line stuck within dialogue. This is one of the signs a script was written by an amateur.

Every parenthetical gets its own line.

(V.O.) AND (O.S.)

Another form of the parenthetical is for "voice-over" and "off-screen." You will sometimes see `O.C.` as opposed to `O.S.` meaning Off Camera.

Either is acceptable, but I always prefer using O.S. because O.C. is usually reserved for sitcom writing.

There's a big difference between off-screen and voice-over, and I see folks confuse them from time to time. Despite being very different, both go in the same place.

These parentheticals go to the right of the character's name.

They do not go within dialogue. They do not get their own lines.

Let's look at Off-Screen first.

Here is the proper use of the Off-Screen parenthetical:

```
                    LARRY
          You don't remember?

                    BRENDA (O.S.)
          I can't hear you!
```

This indicates that Brenda is in the scene, but not currently onscreen. You can use periods or no periods, dealer's choice. (OS) or (O.S.), either is acceptable.

Here's an example of doing it the *wrong* way:

```
                    LARRY
          You don't remember?

                    BRENDA
              (O.S.)
          I can't hear you!
```

I will say the above misplacement isn't overly egregious, and if your writing is great, no one will likely have an issue with it. However, if your writing isn't great then any little thing, like a misplaced parenthetical, will just add to the reader's displeasure.

The Voice-Over parenthetical goes in the same spot as O.S. but means something very different. Where O.S. means the character is in the scene but not onscreen, voice-over means the character is not in the scene.

It's most often used as an omniscient narrator for the story. You'll have a lot of gurus shun using voice-over narration calling it everything from a crutch to a cliché, but let me share even more truth with you . . .

Cliché isn't in the idea, it's in the execution.

Check out the voice-over narration in Jim Uhl's FIGHT CLUB screenplay, or Frank Darabont's Oscar-nominated script for THE SHAWSHANK REDEMPTION. You think those (or any other great screenplays with voice-over narration) would have been better without it?

Let's look at proper V.O. use:

```
                    LARRY
          You don't remember?

                    BRENDA (V.O.)
          I never forget a thing.
```

In this example, Brenda could be dead, in the future, the past, or just simply hanging out in a van with that dude's nephew. Wherever she is, she is not in the scene. The voice-over indicates either Larry or the reader (or both) is hearing Brenda's voice. It's not actually happening in the scene, unless the story is supernatural, and Larry suddenly hears the disembodied voice of his long-lost lover. But that's very specific.

Another common use of voice-over is the internal monologue of a character. Here's a proper example.

```
                    LARRY
          You don't remember?
               (V.O.)
          I know she remembers.
```

This is how to show the reader we HEAR the character (of Larry) thinking.

Don't fear V.O. and O.S. Just know how to use them. And how not to use them.

TRANSITIONS

Transitions are just that—a transition. They are traditionally on the right side of the screenplay (but I've seen them on the left, not a problem) and usually indicate a passage of time or an emphasis on some sort of change. See the following example (**bolded** for our purposes):

```
INT. KITCHEN - DAY

Larry and Brenda sit at the table.

                    LARRY
          You don't remember?

Brenda says nothing. They listen to the rain pepper
the roof.

                    LARRY
              (smiles)
          It was a night like tonight.

Brenda shifts, uncomfortable.

                    LARRY
          I'm not moving until you speak.

                                        DISSOLVE TO:

INT. KITCHEN - NIGHT

Brenda and Larry sit there. Neither has moved. Even
the rain is gone.
```

Another way to do a transition is to simply write LATER. This is best placed on the left side.

```
                    LARRY
          You don't remember?

Brenda just stares . . .

                    LARRY
          I'm not moving until you speak.

LATER

Brenda and Larry sit there. Neither has moved. Even
the rain is gone.
```

Another common transition is `CUT TO`. This is overused by a lot of newer writers. You do not need to put `CUT TO:` between every scene even if your screenwriting software thinks it's a good idea. Please don't do this. Not only does it take up valuable screenplay real estate, but it interrupts the rhythm of the read with needless words.

I will use `SMASH CUT TO:` when I want to emphasize one scene "smashes" into another scene, most often for dramatic or comedic purposes. Example:

```
Brenda shifts, uncomfortable.

                    LARRY
          Damn it, Brenda, give me something here!

                                        SMASH CUT TO:

Larry lies on the floor with a hatchet embedded in
his chest.
```

The above example can be dramatic or comedic depending on the tone of the script. Or both if it's a Coen Brothers tale.

Some writers use "JUMP CUT" for these types of transitions, but I prefer how "smash" looks and feels on the page. Either is acceptable.

The only "rule of formatting" I truly believe is absolute is the one that says every screenplay should be written in 12pt Courier font. Let me adjust that . . . I believe you should print and send in your scripts in 12pt Courier font. You can write them in any font and size you please, just don't ever show or send anything that isn't 12pt Courier. Why? It is just one of those very, very rare rules that is a rule. Don't break it. You may use any variation of Courier: Courier New, Courier Prime, or just good old Courier.

That said, you can use different fonts *within* your script. Many professionals do as Dan Gilroy showed us with NIGHTCRAWLER. Doing this is absolutely allowed and accepted.

Something that I make sure to never do in any of my scripts is to have a page break interrupt a sentence. Ever. This isn't any sort of rule, it's just my personal preference. Be it description, dialogue, whatever, I always have every page of every script end on a period. Sluglines don't have periods. Never position a slugline so there's a page break after it and before the first action line. Doing this just looks amateurish.

PAGE COUNT

Another element of formatting the gurus and charlatans love to shout about is page count.

> **YOUR FEATURE SCRIPT MUST BE UNDER 120 PAGES OR YOU WILL BE KICKED OUT OF SHOW BUSINESS FOREVER!**
>
> **YOUR SPEC DRAMA PILOT MUST BE UNDER 61 PAGES OR YOU WILL NEVER BE ALLOWED TO STREAM ANYTHING EVER AGAIN!**

I'd rather have a rusty shrimp fork stuck in my eye than hear this page count lie ever again.

This type of ridiculous "advice," and I could hardly type the word advice with a straight face, has hurt more screenplays than it ever helped.

Now, due to our society's tragic tumble into mediocrity, I feel compelled to point out the obvious . . .

I am not saying you should write a 246-page feature or a 119-page one-hour pilot and expect people not to shudder.

What I am saying is IF you write an amazing, compelling, entertaining feature script that happens to be more than 120 pages long, it will not matter. So long as the writing is great. If you write a 69-page spec pilot it will not matter IF your writing is great.

Now, there may be some indie producer who's looking for a script to meet a certain (usually very small) budget criterion. In these specific cases, page count may matter because these producers aren't looking for great scripts as much as they're in search of something that fits into the math of their budgets. Within this context, it's much easier to secure financing for a decent 98-page feature than it is for a beautifully written 130-pager.

Getting back to the mainstream Hollywood industry, just as page count won't matter if your writing is brilliant, the reverse is true, and this is where the guru's argument falls completely apart.

If your writing is lousy, it won't matter if your pilot is a lean, mean 54 pages, or your feature is a low fat 101 pages. If it's lousy, it's lousy, and no one will buy it or want to meet with you. I've read sub-100-page features that were so poorly written it felt like I was slogging through 184 pages. I've read 140-page features that were so well written they felt like they were less than 100 pages.

What matters is the QUALITY OF THE WRITING. Writers who are focused on keeping their script under a random number of pages are not focused on writing the best script they can, and it will show. You must write free of any thought of "rules" or coloring inside any random boxes.

You will often hear professional screenwriters talk of cutting pages when we are rewriting. But here's the thing: we don't do it for the sake of page count, we do it for the sake of *the read*. Omitting needless words (see below) often leads to lower page counts. I don't consciously think, "*Oh, this will read better at 114 pages than it will at 117.*"

That's just stupid.

I make the read as great as it can be, and the page count is what it is. If I end up with a screenplay that is 120 pages, and page 120 is only two 8ths of the page long, then yes, I will go in and get it down to 119. Again, not for page count, but for the look and feel. I will do that if my draft is 102 pages, and the last page is only two 8ths long. I don't want my final page to ever be less than half a page. Just another idiosyncrasy of my process. YMMV.

ASIDE: Scripts are broken down by 8ths of page for production. The origin story is pages were generally eight inches long, so production broke them down by inches, thus *8ths*. No other reason than that. It's still done today because, tradition.

If I still haven't convinced you to ignore the page count lie, think of it this way . . . IF page count truly mattered the way the gurus and charlatans claim it matters, then the following scenario would be true:

A producer/studio exec/agent reads your 132-page feature. The writing is some of the best they've read in a long time. They love the characters, the story, and especially your Voice. But they pass on you and your project because it's simply 12 pages over the max. They tell you, "*Damn, if only you had cut twelve pages out of it, you could've won the Oscar, and gotten an overall studio deal with an assistant and parking spot closer than Callie Khouri, but you just can't break the page count rule.*"

Uh, huh.

Same for this scenario: a producer/exec/agent reads your feature screenplay, and the writing is flat, the story sucks, and every character sounds exactly the same. However, it's only 101 pages, so they tell you, "*Your writing is horrible, but you sure nailed that page count rule! We're going to pay you millions to keep writing your terrible, but perfectly page-counted scripts! Gustav, tell Callie to move her car!*"

Any of you who think either scenario could ever play out need to stop reading this book right now and move north to raise snow weasels because your chances of ever having a successful career as a professional screenwriter are less than winning the lottery twice.

Hollywood exists to make money, and good writing is the foundation of Hollywood. Good writing is rarely overlooked for any reason. Great writing is never overlooked.

If your script is great, be it 101 pages or 140 pages, it's going to get noticed and YOU are going to get noticed, and more than likely get a shot at a career as a professional screenwriter. If your writing isn't very good, page count will not save you.

The next thing I want to discuss is Omit Needless Words—a personal rule for my own writing, and something I preach to those I'm mentoring.

But the reason for omitting needless words has NOTHING to do with page count.

I own a t-shirt that says Omit Needless Words. That's how much I believe in it. But not for the reason you think. I believe in Omit Needless Words because when you do, it makes your writing better, which makes the read better.

Take a look at this first example, which is filled with needless words.

```
INT. KITCHEN - DAY

Larry sits in a chair at the kitchen table with a cup
of coffee in his hand. He is waiting for Brenda.

He takes a sip of coffee then sets the cup down. He
looks at his watch and checks the time.
```

Compare that with this:

```
INT. KITCHEN - DAY

Larry sips his coffee . . . checks his watch . . .
waiting . . . for Brenda.
```

Notice how different the *feel* of the read is? When you omit needless words, you can create emotion. Suspense. Tension. Anticipation.

Both examples say the same thing, but the second one does it with thirty-two fewer words, and in doing so actually *adds* tension to the read. Ellipses also help build tension and can be used when you omit needless words.

ONW as the kids call it—actually, the kids don't call it anything, the kids are busy watching videos of that guy pretending to be a bush—is something I never pay attention to when writing my first draft. Omit Needless Words is something for the rewrite. It goes to what I have mentioned before; the rhythm and tone of the read. Needless words slow the read at best and at worst impair the rhythm of your writing.

Another example I think really drives home the Omit Needless Words importance is the infamous short story most often credited to Ernest Hemingway, though, it's been proven he was not the original author—it was from a classified ad in a 1945 Tucson, AZ newspaper.

For sale. Baby shoes. Never used.

Six words that tell a story with a beginning, middle, and end. It also does the most important thing in writing: it elicits an emotional response from the reader. Would anyone have ever heard of this tale if the original ad had read:

For sale: a brand new pair of baby shoes that have never been used.

Which version is more emotional, more compelling?

Omit needless words.

Now, as there are no absolutes in this screenwriting thing, let's take a look at when *more* words improve the writing. Think back to the MICHAEL CLAYTON example from our chapter on Voice. Actually, flip back and read it again. I'll wait.

Sometimes more words, even many more words, make the writing and the read better. That's the takeaway from this . . . do whatever it takes to make THE READ the best it can be.

7

LET'S TALK ABOUT THE S WORD

STRUCTURE.

Structure is the most talked about, yet most MISUNDERSTOOD aspect of screenwriting.

From gurus and charlatans to aspiring scribes, to wannabes, to college professors, to seasoned professionals, everyone talks about structure. And here's the crazy thing . . .

I would estimate at least 90% of the folks you're hearing all this structure talk from are not talking about structure. They think they are, but they are not.

The above statement and this whole chapter are going to be disturbing to some, especially coming from the dude who co-wrote GEOSTORM, so before we continue, I want to drop some cog on you from a couple of screenwriters much better and vastly more successful than myself.

Steve Zaillian, Oscar-winning screenwriter of SCHINDLER'S LIST, SEARCHING FOR BOBBY FISCHER, MONEYBALL, THE IRISHMAN, and more, said:

> *I've never paid any attention to structure, I've relied on inspiration . . . and thought the structure would work itself out. Looking back on things I've done I notice there is a structure to it all I wasn't aware of when I was doing it which makes me think there is simply a natural structure to good storytelling.*

Scott Frank, Oscar nominated screenwriter of MINORITY REPORT, LOGAN, THE QUEEN'S GAMBIT, and countless others, said:

> *"It's an illusion that screenplays are all about structure; that if you can just have the right structure, you can have a good story."*

It. Is. An. Illusion.

Let me tell you once and for all what structure is. Every story from the first bedtime tale read to you to the latest MCU flick has the exact same structure.

Beginning. Middle. End.

That's it.

People will try to convince you that is not true. Why? Because if you know the truth then you have no need for them and whatever they're selling or teaching.

I've even heard working professional screenwriters claim what is most often referred to as "3-Act Structure" (beginning, middle, end) is but just ONE of many types of structure. I know someone who makes a living writing TV movies who claims there are eight different types of structures in screenwriting. This person, like so many others, has confused false "act breaks" with structure.

Academics talk of Shakespeare's 5-Act structure . . . really? Which play did not contain a beginning, middle, and end? I'd love to read it.

Failed professionals (who've written opuses about "Story") have coopted the Shakespeare five-act theory for themselves, calling it "5 Parts." Still others try to convince you there's a 22-step structure, and on, and on.

Lies.

"No, Guyot, you don't get it! What they're saying is a story needs to have all sorts of scenes that contain highs and lows, and conflicts, and surprises and sequences within its beginning, middle, and end!"

Uh, huh. And water is wet.

It is not this mythical "structure" that makes one story flat and uninteresting and another exciting, compelling, thrilling, hilarious, or heartbreaking . . . it's the WRITING.

A screenplay, be it a 30-minute episode of television or a two-and-a-half-hour feature, is not good or bad because of its structure. It is good or bad because of the WRITING. If the writing is good, structure happens.

Let me share some words from my friend Craig Mazin, the brilliant, Emmy-winning screenwriter of CHERNOBYL, THE LAST OF US, and many feature films.

Craig has said the following about structure, and I agree with each statement:

- Structure is a total trap.
- Structure doesn't say, "This happens on this page; this happens on that page; here's a midpoint, etc . . ."
- Structure is not a tool, it is a symptom.
- Structure isn't something you write well, it's something that happens because you wrote well.

Let's repeat that last one and bold it . . .

STRUCTURE ISN'T SOMETHING YOU WRITE WELL, IT'S SOMETHING THAT HAPPENS BECAUSE YOU WROTE WELL.

That sentence right there is why every screenwriting book, every guru and charlatan, every screenwriting professor, all the screenwriting social media accounts, and most other folks talking about structure are wrong.

To quote Mazin one more time: *Structure isn't the dog, it's the tail.*

You do not begin with structure. Structure happens.

Structure happens.

It is a symptom. A result of having told a good story.

To hammer this home one more time, let's revisit Mazin's first quote:

STRUCTURE IS A TOTAL TRAP.

Are you getting this yet? If you're pushing back, ask yourself if you know more about what makes great screenwriting than Zaillian, Frank, Mazin, and all the other Club WPS members who agree with me.

There are only two types of structure:

Structure the verb, and structure the noun. The noun form of "structure" is the one you should concern yourselves with: the "structure of your story." This is the structure that succeeds because of a well written story or fails due to a poorly written one.

But more often than not, folks discuss structure in its verb form *thinking* they're talking about the noun. Or worse, thinking there's no difference between the two.

The *noun* form of structure and the *verb* form are as different as *Telling a LIE, and To LIE down.*

Structure the noun is the one to focus on, and it happens after you write. Not during, and God forbid, not before. To hear from Mazin once again, he equates trying to write your screenplay by starting with structure akin to having a coroner deliver your baby. Sure, they're a doctor, and it might work out okay, but is that really who you want in the delivery room?

When you write a screenplay you start from nothing. A blank page. You are inventing, creating, using your imagination. When you try to do this by starting with thoughts like *This piece must go here; this must happen over here; I must put this thing here,* and so on, you clog your imagination and creative process with so much sludge, so much external thinking, there is no way you are going to be free enough to write your best. Sure, you'll write, you will probably even finish, but the result won't be very good.

Structure happens.

When you meet a friend for coffee or tea because you gotta tell them what happened the night before, do you think about all the structural elements, inciting incidents and low point turns before you tell your story? Of course not. You simply *tell the story*. If it's a good story, structure happens. There will be a beginning, middle, and end with highs and lows, turns, and a conclusion either completely surprising or inevitable, or if you really nailed it, both.

Why would you write a screenplay any differently?

Beginning, middle, end.

If you don't like using those words, then call it Three-Act structure, or Setup, Conflict, Resolution. Call it Story Structure, or Wanda the Magical Structure Maiden. Call it whatever the heck you want, but that is literally all you need to know before you sit down to tell your tale. Thinking about anything beyond that will simply block your imagination, and while you may pull off what appears to be a beautifully structured screenplay, I guarantee you it will be flat, unoriginal, and sound exactly like all the other beautifully structured flat, unoriginal screenplays written the same way.

Now, some might think, *"Wait a sec. Structuring your story* (VERB: *building, designing, etc.) is every bit as important as the noun, and every writer must learn to do it properly!"*

Umm, with all due respect...

Nope.

Here's the thing . . .

Structure the verb is unique to every writer.

I won't bother with another *Let's repeat that*. Just reread the above sentence.

The way a screenwriter structures their story is unique to each writer. Ah, I repeated it, didn't I? Couldn't help myself. It's that important.

Despite what the books and gurus claim, there is no correct or incorrect way to do it.

The way I construct a story is different from the way Eric Heisserer does it, or Issa Rae, or Kwan & Scheinert. How Aline Brosh McKenna designs her stories is different from Sterlin Harjo or Charlie Kaufman. I've heard Aaron Sorkin speak in detail about how he structures (verb) his stories. I can't do it his way because my brain and who I am as a person and storyteller is very different than Sorkin.

Sure, when we're all hanging out at the Farmer's Market swapping our latest soul-crushing rejection stories, we will invariably find certain aspects of our processes to be similar. But no two are alike.

This is why all the white noise from the gurus about HOW to do it is useless. We are all unique individual artists and storytellers, and when you try to build/construct/create your story using someone else's method, you're making it harder on yourself than necessary.

I know there are folks who believe good screenwriting is math. Just follow the equations. I believe they are wrong. Because it isn't the math of a screenplay that makes one great and one awful. It's the emotion, the heart, the imagination, the writing.

That said, if a screenwriter's brain works best doing the math first, good on them. But they're in the minority.

I try never to use the word structure when discussing the verb form. I will say "build" or "create" or "design," because then there's much less confusion. When I am building a story, it starts with a simple idea, which might be a character, situation, experience, or some sort of dilemma. Often, it's a *What if?* scenario. Even when I'm writing a math-heavy type of story, like a heist script (as you'll see later), I must always find the simple emotional journey for the character. It is all about character. Plot doesn't exist without character (Graham Yost's SPEED notwithstanding), so the only way to make some super cool "plot" work is for it to be experienced by compelling, interesting characters with even more compelling, interesting relationships.

When I wrote and produced LEVERAGE for TNT, we had a heist or con in every episode, and thanks to the brilliance of our showrunner, John Rogers, they were usually incredibly complex and required a lot of "math." However, not one episode of that series would have ever worked if it had not been for the characters and their relationships with each other. That's what drove our stories.

Nowhere from the beginning stages of an idea through the outline to the writing do I ever think about inciting incidents or midpoint turns or progressive complications or "storming the castle." Insert eyeroll emoji. No good working professional screenwriter does. Those things will happen organically if I do my job as a storyteller.

Structure happens.

All the placement of the *inciting incidents* and *midpoint turns* and *progressive complications* is for when you're finished and the gurus and professors are doing forensic analysis on your script because what you wrote won all the awards.

Yes, things must happen in your story. Changes must occur within characters and their relationships. But those *things* are rarely what you think they *must* be. Look at the 1981 film MY DINNER WITH ANDRE by Wallace Shawn & Andre Gregory. It's 108 minutes of two dudes talking over dinner. Yet, the story has just as many changes, highs and lows, turns and surprises as does the latest action thriller starring Hollywood's Clean & Jerk of the moment.

Wait, what?

AUTHOR'S NOTE: Don't ever use phrases like "Wait, what?" in your scripts. It's tired, out of date, and just lazy writing.

Yes. If you read the script for MY DINNER WITH ANDRE, it's easy to think there's no inciting incident or midpoint turns or any of the other guru garbage . . . but there is. It's just not what and where the gurus tell you it must be, and more importantly, it wasn't written that way. The dinner itself IS the inciting incident. And by the end of the story the main character, Wally, is changed from the beginning of the story because his relationship with the other character has changed. These highs and lows, these changes don't have to be giant tentpole types of things. They can be small, in fact, for me, the smaller the better. It's more intimate, more visceral.

What I am saying here is the same thing Zaillian and Mazin and Waller-Bridge, et al, say, and that is thinking about these movements, these ups and downs, twists and turns, in the sense of, *"I must have one here, and another one here"* as opposed to letting them happen organically as you take your characters on an emotional journey with each other, will cause you to write a tail wagging the dog script. The moment you move from the art of storytelling to the math of forensic analysis *before* you finish, you are doomed to write just another flat, unoriginal script.

Even when my *What if?* moment is an incident that incites action, I'm not consciously thinking of it like that. I'm thinking about character, emotion, and relationships.

I know it's tough to buy into all this new structure stuff when some of you are looking at my produced credits and going, "*This guy?*" Fair. So, let me repeat what Scott Frank said . . . *It's an illusion to think having the right structure leads to a good story.*

The truth is a good story leads to a well-structured script.

Structure happens.

Now, please pay close attention to this next bit . . .

You know that thing you read on every screenwriting website and hear from every screenwriting guru about, "*You gotta grab them in the first ten pages!*" or they'll stop reading. Which, in the last couple of years—due to our shortening attention spans—has now become, "*You gotta grab them in the first FIVE pages!*"

Both are wrong.

Here for the first time ever, is the TRUTH about what grabs a reader in the early pages of a screenplay:

Good writing.

Nothing has to blowup, there doesn't have to be some crazy surprise or twist, good writing is what grabs a reader and keeps them turning pages. I've read countless scripts where the poor screenwriter tried to grab me in the first few pages by doing some version of the above . . . it didn't grab me because it didn't work because the writing sucked. It doesn't matter what blows up or what crazy twist or shocking incident you throw into your early pages if your writing is not good. Inciting incidents, twists and turns, surprises, and saving domesticated moggies does not make good writing. It can enhance good writing, but good writing isn't born from it.

When I am building a story, I'm focused on characters and their relationships, and what is the most interesting, intriguing, entertaining, compelling way to express the **simple emotional journey**. I have made the mistake of writing something by not doing that, and as you'll see later, it cost me.

The most mechanical I ever get during the structure-the-verb phase is thinking about dilemma. Conflict. Choices. That's why it's perfectly acceptable to refer to structure-the-noun as "Setup, Conflict, Resolution."

There's more to come in this chapter, but if you want to skip ahead because you have to be at Great White in an hour to show your pitch deck to a producer you met online, here's a summary:

Don't overthink. In fact, don't think at all.

Did you ever see ENTER THE DRAGON? Starring the late Bruce Lee? While he doesn't have a writing credit on the film, he wrote more than half of it, including a couple of scenes that connect with this whole screenwriting thing. My favorite is when his character is speaking to a pupil. They could've been discussing screenwriting as opposed to martial arts:

> *Don't think. Feel. It is like a finger pointing the way to the moon. Don't concentrate on the finger or you'll miss all that heavenly glory.*

Enjoy your dinner. Forget the pitch deck.

People desperately want there to be some secret "hack" to good screenwriting. Because (again) they've been indoctrinated for decades that there IS some secret hack when the truth is all that's really required to tell a good story is to put a lot of work into writing your way in your own Voice.

When folks try to make screenwriting more complex than it really is, they take what we naturally do as storytellers and turn it into some combination of IKEA instructions for assembling a storage bed and a Navajo language enchiridion. It's what every How-To book is about. They turn beginning, middle, and end into some labor-intensive process of putting twenty-some steps within your story, or placing certain actions at certain points, all in an effort to convince you there's some special sauce, and they'll happily give you the recipe for a price.

If you talk to the best chefs in the world, most will tell you the fewer ingredients the better the result.

It is a lie that the quality of a screenplay is all about the construction. It is all about the writing.

If you write a great story filled with compelling characters and relationships, you will end up with something that has inherent dilemma and conflict, twists and turns, surprises, and all the other stuff that creates an emotional response in the reader and thus, is considered well-structured.

How do you do this? By writing. And writing. And rewriting. And rewriting.

Now, take a breath because here's some more truth that not only goes against ALL you've been taught, but is something you've never read in any screenwriting book, or heard from any screenwriting guru. Ready?

Just as structure-the-verb is unique to each writer, so is structure-the-noun.

Yes, that all-important "Three-Act Structure," "Beginning, middle, end," and "Structure happens" stuff is unique to each writer.

"What??? Come on, Guyot!"

It's true.

Every writer builds their stories differently and as a result, every writer's story is different. If you take ten working professional screenwriters and have them all write a script from the same logline, you will get ten totally different scripts. Every script's structure (noun) will be unique, meaning, where the beginning of the story flows into the middle, and the middle moves into the end won't be the same for any of the scripts. The moments of surprise, conflict, or dilemma will all happen at different places and in different ways.

Now, here's the truly amazing part of this reality . . . because of that, the structure-the-noun of the story will be different for every reader!

I know you're hyperventilating but stay with me here.

How we build and then write our stories are as unique as we are. Great screenwriters write their stories their way in their own Voice, while mediocre ones (or worse) write stories by trying to copy someone else's way of doing it. Often it's someone who's never written a good screenplay in their life.

If you're having trouble wrapping your mind around what I'm saying, try this: ask anyone where the first act ends in JAWS or either of the first two GODFATHERS (or any other film for that matter), and you'll spark debate.

Because it's not binary, it's emotional.

One person may feel like Act One in JAWS ends with the Kitner boy. Another person may feel like it's absolutely when the sheriff who's afraid of water learns there's a shark out there. Even professional screenwriters debate these things. It's one of the fun things we do when we get together, other than discussing food. It's different for each viewer of each film and each reader of each script because the writer wrote it their way instead of trying to write it by adhering to certain "structural rules" imposed by some third party.

My point is it doesn't matter. Okay, it matters, but not in the way you think it does.

Just write your story. Plan, research, sketch, do beat sheets, Gregorian chants, outlines, or none of those things, whatever is your process. Think about the simple emotional journey. How you can create dilemma for your characters and their relationships; the Conflict of *Setup, Conflict, Resolution*. Think about the central dramatic argument driving your story. Think about the language of your script. Your syntax, your turns of phrase. The writing. And most importantly, think about the why.

Then type FADE IN: and keep going until you type FADE OUT.

Don't bury yourself in the elephant grass of plot points and inciting incidents and what happens on what page. That is death to creativity. Write your story from your gut. From your heart. From your soul. And keep going until you type FADE OUT. Even when it feels like it sucks, and trust me, it is going to suck! Just keep going.

Folks talk about doing the "vomit draft." Getting it out as fast as you can. I don't like that term because it implies you haven't done any prep work. If you've done your prep properly (your "mise en place" for my chefs out there), your first draft won't have to feel like you're barfing up your story. It will suck as all first drafts do, but it will be the foundation from which your best story emerges during the rewrites. And the rewriting will be easier if you've done your prep work.

Finish the first draft, step away for a while, then go back and read the thing and see how it feels. Don't check to see if you hit some cat-saving beat in the proper place, but see how it FEELS. Is it resonating on an emotional level? Is your language interesting and engaging? Forget all the math because I swear on the scripts of Alvy Sargent it will take care of itself as you go.

I can tell some of you are shaking right now. Relax. Breathe. I understand how difficult it is to buy into something when you've been indoctrinated into the exact opposite for decades. Just remember to always *consider the source* before taking any screenwriting advice. Is it from someone who tried and failed? Someone who had very brief success, but couldn't keep their card? Is it from someone who calls themselves an expert despite never having written a screenplay? Or someone who has been paid to do it year after year, and is still doing it successfully? Like Steve Zaillian, Scott Frank, or Craig Mazin?

Bulls in the bullring, remember?

The gurus want you to believe screenwriting is complex and dense, so you're afraid and feel like you need a guide, a shaman, someone just like themselves to lead you through the darkness.

The gurus claim the evidence that proves their opinions is in analyzing the product after the fact. Breaking down a finished screenplay or film and pointing out the 22 steps, or the kitty beats, or whichever Kool-Aid they drank. But again, there has never been one great script written that way, while there have been millions of awful ones.

You learn to write by writing. You get better with every page you write. Every scene. Every script. You do not get better by following charts or formulas or graphs.

"You still don't get it, Guyot, those books may not be for working professionals, but they're really helpful for people just starting out!"

That's another lie. These books and gurus and rules are absolutely terrible for folks just starting out. Here's why . . .

Forgive me for making one last golf analogy but consider this: if you are taught to play wrong, to swing poorly, and you practice that way every day for a year, you will not be a better golfer. You will be a year worse than you were before because you will have been grooving bad habits.

Same with screenwriting. If you write every day for a year, but you're writing the way all the failures and poseurs tell you to write, you are only grooving bad writing habits. However, if you write every day for a year, focusing on telling your story your way in your Voice, you will be a much, much better writer than when you began.

This is probably where a few of you are thinking, "*Oh, yeah? What about Dan Harmon's Story Circle??? He's way more successful than you and that's how HE does it!*"

As I've said more than once here, there are no absolutes. Regarding Harmon's Story Circle, I'll say this: I don't know Dan, never met him. I do know people who know him and have been told more than once he created the Story Circle thing almost as a middle finger to studio and network executives who were constantly giving him terrible notes on things they knew nothing about. Maybe Dan does use his Circle before he writes anything? Or maybe he uses it as an example for network execs to comprehend his episodic television creations? The little I do know about the man is that the writers who influenced him were definitely not folks who wrote by putting the tail before the dog.

If you want to write following a circle chart because Dan Harmon says to, good on ya. Best of luck! Hopefully, you possess some of the massive talent Dan has, otherwise, it's going to be a slog.

I'm trying to help those of you who (like me) don't have Dan's level of talent. And the best chance we have is forgetting all the charts and graphs and formulas, filling our minds instead with as much imagination, inspiration, faith, and trust as possible and then writing. Then rewriting and rewriting.

"Okay, Guyot, so what are we supposed to do when it comes to all this structure stuff? How do we make sure our script is structured (verb) properly if we don't start with that?"

There's an old aphorism from the cycling world:

> How do you know if the weather is too bad to ride? Go out and ride, and when you get back, you'll know.

Write your script your way. When you're done, you'll know if it's structured properly. One of the best ways to tell if you have a strongly structured script is if you don't notice the "structure." If it doesn't jump out at you.

Sidney Lumet told me (during that same Niagara weekend), *"If you notice my directing in a film, then I've failed as a storyteller."*

The same goes for all this structure talk.

If your structure doesn't work that means YOUR STORY doesn't work. So, go back and fix it. But you won't fix it by placing some inciting incident on some certain page or making sure you have a second plot point between the midpoint turn and the whatever. You fix it by feel. By tone. By rhythm. By emotion. By language. By making sure it's written in a compelling, interesting way.

I think another reason so many newer screenwriters feel the need to be obsessive about structure is because they listen to podcasts or watch videos where working professional screenwriters talk about some movie or series they wrote, and tell the story of some Act Three problem which they had to fix just before shooting, and it turned out it was actually an Act One problem, and they had to perform all this literary triage to the "structure" to fix the problem.

Wow, that was a quality run-on sentence.

Working professional screenwriters often talk about structure-the-verb when interviewed because they don't stop to think the folks listening or reading will likely confuse it with structure-the-noun. They can talk in those terms because they know what they're doing. I can talk structure all day long with other screenwriters. Or with directors, producers, executives. I can seamlessly transition from the verb to the noun and back. Most of us can.

But we don't write the way we talk. That's just shop talk.

Writing movies inside the studio system is a different animal than writing your first script on spec. There's a language that screenwriters need to speak when dealing with executives, directors, producers, and the like. It's a magic act—we perform an illusion. We spew all this mechanical, non-imaginative speak for the powers that be, then go back to our desks and we write the way we write.

Structure happens.

But hey, I will tell you this; if you'd rather follow all these "structure rules" it will be easier to write your script. It's always easier when you follow a set of instructions rather than make your own way. The result will be one of two things: you will write a well-structured bad script. Or you'll write a fine script that sounds just like hundreds of others. Neither will get you into Club WPS.

Listen, I understand. When you've been struggling just to finish your first screenplay, when you're completely confused because it seems like such a specific and foreign way of writing, and then you read a book that tells you just follow these steps, or this formula and you will have a script. So, you do it, and VOILA! You really DO have a finished script! Holy Helvetica, that book was amazing! It helped me finish my script!

While finishing a screenplay puts you ahead of many wannabes, doing so has NOTHING to do with whether it's any good. I would argue a first draft written by someone telling a story in their own Voice their own way will be generally better than a fourth or fifth draft of a script written by someone who is following all the Dos and Do Nots.

If your script isn't working after you've finished it, look at your characters and their relationships. Look at how you're telling the story—not with structure, but with language. How is the story WRITTEN? Are your action lines flat, boring, just reporting of what's in the scene, or are they alive, evocative, and engaging? Is the writing focused on your characters' relationships with each other, and how those relationships inform and affect the story? Is there an emotional journey taking place? Is your dialogue authentic and/or engaging and full of subtext, or is it on the nose, wooden, and full of exposition? Do you have way too many parentheticals with adverbs ending in LY?

So often we're told to focus on the wrong things when our script isn't working. The best showrunners I've worked with (Barbara Hall, John Rogers, Hart Hanson) always had their writers focus on the story via the writing. What does that mean? It means, they never talked about midpoints and second-act turns, and blah, blah, blah. It was always about improving the writing. How simply describing a scene differently or changing a character's POV could improve not just the scene, but the overall story. If the payoff of a character's story wasn't working, they didn't go back and look at the setup or inciting incident, etc. They looked at the writing. Is the dialogue doing its job? Is the characters' behaviors and responses on point with the emotional journey of the story?

As I've said, I've read plenty of scripts that had good, solid "structure," but were terrible reads because the writing wasn't good.

Structure happens.

Your First Act (Beginning) can be whatever length you make it. Your Second Act (Middle) can be exceedingly long or very short, depending on how you are telling your story and what type of story it is. Your Third Act (End) can be five pages or thirty-five pages, so long as it resolves your setup and conflict in some satisfying way. You can do it however you want so long as the WRITING is good.

The gurus and charlatans will scream it is an absolute atrocity to say a third act can be five or thirty-five pages, or a first act can end on page 50. Just remember what I said earlier—structure is unique to each reader because it is unique to each writer.

Focus on the language, the writing. Don't focus on the math. Not only will your script be better for it, but you will become a better writer faster.

Here's another truth bomb . . . you already know how to do all this!

You have been sucking up narrative your entire life. You DO NOT have to *learn* story. You already know it. Every episode of television you've watched, every movie, every novel or short story you've read, every tale you've heard from friends or family, every story YOU have told, it's all narrative. All this story stuff is already in your brain. You have been evaluating, deciphering, and absorbing story since your parents read you *Goodnight Moon,* which is the GODFATHER II of all picture books; terribly structured yet still works brilliantly!

You know what works and what doesn't. What causes you to turn to your partner after you've binged four episodes in a row, and go, "*Just one more!*" You know what causes you to flip the channel on something after five or ten minutes, or finish watching a film and go, "*That's two hours I'll never get back!*"

The books and gurus will tell you all the things your story must contain for it to be compelling or entertaining, and hey, here is where I'll say they are (more or less) on point. You do want highs and lows, you do want surprises and turns, and all the other things that make stories interesting. But again, if you put the cart full of all those things so far ahead of your horse named Story, you're going to write a bad script.

Stop believing there is a hack. There is no hack.

"STORY STRUCTURE"

Something else you'll hear a lot about is "story structure." Folks love to throw around the term story structure when it comes to screenplays as if it's something different than simple structure. The next time you hear all this story structure talk pay attention to how much talk there is about THE WRITING. Story structure is no different from stuff we've already discussed. It's just another fancy term. So, why is there so much talk about it? For the same reason there's so much talk about structure in general: you don't have to know a thing about being a good writer if it's really all about structure.

Story is part of writing. Duh. But I will stand firm in my belief the better writer you are, the better storyteller you are. And I say that knowing of folks like Dan Brown and Colleen Hoover; prose authors who have sold millions upon millions of books without having any real writing talent.

But they sure as heck know how to tell a good STORY. I wish I could tell stories like Colleen Hoover.

Unfortunately, the screenwriting world is much different from the prose world. Yes, you could perhaps get your Club WPS card by writing a screenplay with a great story and mediocre writing. But you likely won't hang onto that card for long. The powers that be will buy your script, fire you, and bring on someone who IS a good writer. You may get another gig or even sell another great story/mediocre writing script. But the same thing will happen, and before you know it, you'll be sitting around that creepy Starbucks in Toluca Lake telling stories about that brief time YOU were in Club WPS.

There's a reason the author of the cat books sold more pitches than he ever did screenplays.

You can tell a good story without being a good writer. You know many people who fall into this category. Like that one cousin who shows up at Thanksgiving every year with their tales about how they and their buddy, Cherokee Hank, came so close to making it rich, if not for a few variables they failed to consider!

Good stories are great. A good story within a screenplay is great! A good story within a well-written screenplay is GOLD!

More truth:

A well-written screenplay with a weak story will get you more meetings and give you a better shot at success than a poorly written screenplay with a seemingly great story.

Again, I'm not here to help you sell something, I'm here to help give you the best shot at a CAREER as a Working Professional Screenwriter.

NONLINEAR STORYTELLING

Here's another term they love to drop on you because it makes them sound wicked smart. Nonlinear storytelling/structure/narrative; whatever label you want to give it. The uninformed love to give examples of nonlinear screenplays as proof that I am wrong about structure. PULP FICTION, BARBARIAN, CITIZEN KANE, OPPENHEIMER (and most every other Nolan script), and all the others are considered screenplays that "*break the rules* of traditional structure!"

Wrong.

Please tell me which of those screenplays did not have a beginning, middle, and end? Which did not contain a SETUP, followed by a CONFLICT, followed by a RESOLUTION?

Writing your story in a nonlinear way has ZERO to do with the structure (noun) of your story. Did OPPENHEIMER not have a proper Setup? Was there not a boatload of Conflict in the middle? Was there not a Resolution at the end?

Nonlinear storytelling is a type of STORYTELLING. It is not a type of structure.

THE HERO'S JOURNEY

Oh, how the gurus love The Hero's Journey! It's right up there with breathing. And tacos. Let's drop some more truth bombs . . .

The Hero's Journey is NOT structure. It is a template (a formula) for certain mythological stories. It was popularized by Joseph Campbell in his 1949 book, *The Hero with a Thousand Faces.* Fun fact about old Joe's book: it was never intended as a How-To book on writing. It was more or less about analyzing religions.

Enter Chris Vogler. A low-level Disney exec in the 1980s. In an effort to gain the attention of upper-level execs—who promoted and encouraged the culture of memos within the company—Vogler wrote a memo that basically said, "Folks should read Campbell's book." It pointed out the template (not structure) of certain mythological stories from various cultures. He took Campbell's *The Hero with a Thousand Faces* and wrote what was akin to a high school book report. Vogler claims the memo was so popular within the industry that it took on a life of its own, becoming a tsunami of storytelling genius all aspired to. This has never been verified. At all.

In the early 90s, Vogler turned his book report into his own book, *The Writer's Journey: Mythic Structure for Storytellers and Screenwriters*. Again, despite the word structure being in his title, what he was selling was not structure. That's how much he knew about writing.

The book didn't sell too well, so several years later he updated the references in it and changed the title to *The Writer's Journey: Mythic Structure for Writers*, thinking it would open it up to buyers outside of the screenwriting world. It did. The book became a bestseller, and everyone started (mistakenly) using it to "structure" their stories. All stories. Even ones that had nothing to do with heroes journeying through mythological templates. Guess what? Those screenplays weren't any good and didn't launch any careers.

I have heard people discuss The Hero's Journey ad nauseam, always breaking down finished films and cramming them into their forensic schematics after the fact, claiming this was HOW those films were written. It's funny, but also sad, because I know there are newer screenwriters out there who get duped into believing it's how one writes quality screenplays. It is not.

As Tony Gilroy has said, "*I don't think in archetypes, ever, I think about people. Real people. There are no archetypes.*"

Archetypes came from Carl Jung in the context of discussing dreams. Campbell took that and applied it to cultures and religions. Vogler took that and applied it to writing. If you want to try and write your screenplay thinking The Hero's Journey first, instead of letting other folks do it after your script has been turned into a blockbuster movie, good on ya. But you're making it much, much tougher on yourself, and chances are the result won't be that good.

THE WHY

I debated putting this in the Structure chapter—it sort of feels like it should be somewhere else. But in thinking about it, I realized it is directly connected to all this technical talk of structure.

The gurus love the HOW. How to write, how to structure, how to, how to, how to . . . none of them ever talk about WHY. Why must you write this script? Why do you feel the desire to write this script? Why should you write it in this tone or rhythm? Why are these particular characters in this particular story? Why are they making the choices they make? Why is this story screaming to be told?

The Why is directly connected to our storytelling, but those who don't/can't do it are not conscious of that. They look at screenwriting with binary eyes, only seeing the surface, the math, the linear. They see the tip of the iceberg—the finished product—and think that's it. But we know, just as Rose and Jack knew, the largest and most important part of the iceberg is well under the surface.

If that 5% sticking out of the water is your finished on-screen product, the other 95% consists of everything from the moment you first formed your idea. All the research, sketching, beat sheets, outlines, all the characters and their relationships, why your characters talk and move the way they do, what they don't say and why they don't say it. The conflict, dilemma, the language you write with, the way you engage the reader with everything from a character's glance to your turn of phrase when describing a setting. The rhythm and tone of your words.

The unique way you elicit an emotional response from the reader.

The writing and the rewriting.

You cannot create any sort of emotion without WHY. Why are you writing this story, and why are your characters making the choices they're making? Why is a scene set in a particular location? Why is the story set during a particular time? Why does this story mean something to you? Why are you compelled to tell it?

If you focus on the Why you will be ahead of the game. The more you can create an emotional response in yourself, the more likely your script will do the same for your reader.

One of the things I do early on whenever I write something is create what amounts to a mission statement. The WHY of the project, and why it's worth all the work and effort and frustration I'm about to put myself through. It's been something which has aided me greatly on those days of self-loathing and imposter syndrome when I think the only thing worse than my idea is my talent level. I can go back to that mission statement and find my True North again.

THOSE VEXING "ACT BREAKS" WHEN IT COMES TO TELEVISION WRITING

The last section of this chapter is for those of you who want to write television.

Act Breaks in broadcast television shows are not Act Breaks at all but exist solely to sell ad time. Whether we're talking about sitcoms or one-hour dramas, these "Act Breaks" are manufactured and have zero to do with screenwriting or storytelling or Three-Act Structure. They are pauses in the final cut of the episode so companies can sell their products.

Back when writing television specs was the only way to get a job interview for a staff position . . . wait, let's pause here.

There are two uses of the word "spec."

The first and most common is "spec script" which means a script you have written on your own, without anyone paying you. Spec is short for speculation. You are writing a script on speculation that it will be good enough someone will want to buy it or hire you as a screenwriter. When you hear talk of "spec sales" it means scripts written like this, which some producer or studio purchased.

The other type of "spec" is used exclusively in television and refers to a spec version of an existing show. Until the last few years, the main way a writer got an opportunity to join the staff of a series was to write a "spec" of some current show. The screenwriter was (hopefully) very familiar with the show, and wrote their own idea of an episode, doing their best to capture the tone and feel of the show through the characters' behaviors and voices.

The first script I wrote that really made an impact in Hollywood was a spec episode of a very popular series called NYPD BLUE. I was rather obsessed with that show as a young aspiring screenwriter, and by the grace of God managed to come up with a great story for an episode, while also doing a decent job with the characters. That script led to my first three screenwriting gigs, and it was still getting passed around town a few years after I'd written it, still leading to meetings and pitches.

These days, the only place where a writer will need a spec of an existing television show is for the various fellowships offered by studios and networks. Showrunners of today aren't interested in reading specs of other shows. Nowadays, the most desired screenwriting talent showrunners are searching for is Voice. Showrunners, and most intelligent executives, want to see original material—pilots, plays, etc.—that showcase the writer's own Voice, and reveals their ability to tell a good story, develop characters, etc.

Okay, where were we? Oh yes, those false "Act Breaks" . . .

Back when writing television specs was the only way to get a possible job interview for a staff position on a show, the whole Act Break thing became a big deal. If you were writing a spec episode of any show on broadcast or basic cable, you had to nail the Act Breaks.

Some shows had four act breaks per episode. Some had five. I once worked on a series that had five per episode one season, and the following season we were informed the network had sold more ad time, and we now had to write in SIX act breaks per episode.

Let me tell you, it does not help the writing process.

Having to break up the flow of your story with false act breaks is a massive pain in the writer's tuchus, and it's a big reason why television writing accolades have gone more and more to streaming or premium cable series. Yes, the writing is great on a lot of the broadcast and basic cable shows, but I can't tell you how much it helps the storytelling when you don't have to falsely stop through the script again and again.

Talking exclusively about one-hour shows here (sorry, sitcom writers), when you look at the genuine structure of the script for a random episode of broadcast television, by the time you get to what is the transition from the *actual* Act One of the story (the beginning) to the Act Two (the middle), you may have already had two or sometimes three commercial breaks. And networks are so terrified of people changing channels during the commercials, they force the writers to create false cliffhanger moments which causes more storytelling issues.

I can't confirm whether the following is true, because I heard it secondhand, but supposedly Matt Weiner had his writers on MAD MEN write their scripts without any false breaks—leaving it up to the editing room since it wasn't part of the real writing process. I want it to be true and hope it's true. Whether the story's true or apocryphal, if you watch the series, you can certainly see they didn't give a damn where those false breaks happened. Sometimes the commercial break would come literally in the middle of a scene. A character would speak, and before the other character responds, the show goes to commercial. Then comes right back to the point where we left off. Or a break would come at the end of a scene with nothing close to a cliffhanger or *What happens next???* moment. It was one of the reasons the writing on that series was so pure, and why I loved it as a viewer.

So, how does all this information apply to those of you who have yet to work on a television writing staff?

I always encourage writers to never put act breaks in their spec pilots. Whether you are writing a one-hour drama, or half-hour (single camera) comedy, I believe it's in your best interest to leave out all act breaks.

No "cold open," no "teaser," no "Act 4," none of that.

The reason is threefold. First, so much of the television landscape today is streaming and/or commercial-free, that false act breaks have become a dinosaur of formatting. You don't want your original pilot to look or feel dated.

Second, the showrunner or whomever is reading and judging your writing ability, may disagree with where you put those false breaks. They may think you totally missed the mark, and even if there were parts of your writing they enjoyed, anything that leaves a negative thought in your reader's mind isn't good.

Third, dropping false act breaks into your story hurts your writing. You want your script to be the very best it can be before it gets into the hands of readers who can hire you and/or help your career. Adding false breaks in the story will not lead to it being the best it can be. Try imagining you are writing your pilot for HBO or Netflix, even if you think it's perfect for CBS.

There are few guarantees in life, but I can absolutely guarantee you the following:

There will NEVER be a showrunner or legit producer who reads your script and loves it, loves your writing, but says, "*Well, this writer is great, but I'm not going to meet with them because they didn't have any act breaks in their script.*"

That will never happen.

You know what does happen?

Structure happens.

8

DIALOGUE

THIS CHAPTER WON'T be too long because I am one who believes writing great dialogue cannot be taught. Not by a book, not by a guru, not even by a working professional screenwriter. The writers we feel write the best dialogue are said to have "an ear" for it. How did that phrase come into existence? Because writers who pen the best dialogue are the best listeners. You want to improve your dialogue writing? Improve your listening skills.

As writers of screen or prose, most of us are observers. We observe life. We observe fellow humans; their behavior, their movement . . . their dialogue. We naturally absorb what we hear, and it gets processed through our writer filter, and comes out later within the pages of our scripts.

There are various types of great dialogue writing. There's the heightened reality dialogue of screenwriters like Aaron Sorkin or Tarantino. People don't talk like the characters in their scripts, yet their dialogue is universally acclaimed.

Another one is Scott Rosenberg. The thing that made me fall in love with Rosenberg's writing was the way he wrote dialogue. Again, real people don't talk like his characters, but his dialogue is nothing short of brilliant. Rosenberg's dialogue writing is so great and such a part of his Voice, it is referred to in Hollywood as "Scottspeak." His characters say the cool things we all wish we could say. They toss out those types of amazing lines we think of saying three weeks after the conversation, when we're in the shower replaying what we shoulda said for the twentieth time.

QT is renowned for his dialogue. Love it or hate it, it has amazing aspects to it, and is 100% his own unique Voice. Many have tried to emulate the way he writes dialogue, but no one can. Back in the day, some folks would say Rosenberg was trying to write like QT. The ridiculousness of that statement is barely worth mentioning, but here's the thing . . . had Scott's movies made the money QT's did, and vice-versa, everyone would've said QT was trying to write like Scott. Also, anyone who knows the first thing about screenwriting knows the dialogue written by those two writers is nothing like the other because their Voices are nothing like each other. I was once asked what I thought the difference was between the two, and my response was something like, *"Rosenberg writes with literary intelligence and an understanding of human behavior, while Tarantino writes with neither."* I don't mean that as shade toward QT in the least. He is a great writer, and his dialogue is by far his strongest asset. But he writes from a place nowhere near where Rosenberg writes from. QT was formed on movies, Rosenberg was formed on literature, and the difference is clear in their writing.

Debora Cahn, Tony Gilroy, and Paul Thomas Anderson are screenwriters worth reading to hear what's considered authentic dialogue, meaning dialogue that does sound the way real people speak.

Shonda Rhimes writes fantastic dialogue which possesses the rare combo platter: at times heightened but also incredibly authentic.

Whether you're talking about heightened Sorkinian dialogue or the authenticity of Gilroy or Cahn, there is an attribute both styles have in common, and it's what sets all great dialogue apart from the rest.

Subtext.

There is simply no great dialogue without subtext. Not simply because it's how most of us truly communicate, but because what is implied or beneath the surface—what is not said—is far more interesting and compelling than what is said.

In dialogue, subtext is everything. Whether your characters sing flowery, poetic words or spit uneducated, grammar-challenged ramblings, you must write with inherent subtext if you want your dialogue to be as good as it can be.

So, what about those story situations where exposition needs to come out of a character? That's part of the gig. Especially in television. Instead of having a man with a hat (see the glossary) come out and explain to the reader what's happening, there are ways to get out exposition without it sounding like exposition. One of the best ways to do it is with behavior rather than dialogue.

Say you have a straight, male character who the reader needs to know is thinking about cheating on his wife. You can have him sit at the bar with his buddy and say some version of, "*Every time a woman walks by me, I think about sleeping with her.*"

Don't write that.

Instead, write it without any dialogue. The same two guys are at the bar talking, and a woman walks by. The guy who's thinking about cheating on his wife leans back and checks her out as she passes. When she looks back, their eyes meet. And we know what he's thinking.

Subtext.

Bonus points if the conversation at the bar is subtext as well. They can be discussing sports, and the guy thinking about cheating is saying how there's a player who's been a star for a long time, but isn't as good as they once were, and if the owner would only trade the old war horse in for some super talented young kid, the team might not be in the basement of the standings.

As I look at what I just typed, I want to rewrite it. I don't need the guy to lock eyes with the woman . . . he just needs to watch her go by.

Subtext.

For me, one of the truly great scenes in cinematic history is the last scene in the 1996 film BIG NIGHT, written by Stanley Tucci and Joey Tropiano. The last five minutes of the film contains not a single word of dialogue, but perfectly resolves the setup and conflict of the entire movie. So many writers would have felt the need to say something in this scene. And every studio executive would have all but demanded the need for dialogue. Lots of dialogue. But Tucci and Tropiano wrapped up the movie's story with the most beautiful, elegant, authentic scene of subtext I have ever seen. Go watch it, and then read the script. You'll see what's on screen is exactly what was written . . . and not written.

Omit Needless Words indeed.

My best advice for writing dialogue is in lock step with my advice about structure and everything else we've discussed to this point . . . don't think. Don't *try* to write good dialogue. Don't *try* to write cool things. Don't *try* to write what you think you should write.

As hippie-dippie as it sounds, let your characters write their own dialogue. If you have created multi-dimensional, authentic, compelling characters, let them lead you.

When I'm reading a script one thing that tells me immediately the writer has a long way to go to get better is if their characters all sound the same. My litmus test is something I heard Robert Towne say he always did: if I remove the characters' names from above the dialogue, would I know who is speaking?

I give my own scripts this test during my rewrite phase.

Too many times I read scripts where (again) the writer is trying so hard to color inside the guru lines they pay no attention to the dialogue beyond simply reporting the story. They think adding exclamation points or parentheticals is character work.

Look at your scripts. If you can't tell who's talking without their name above the dialogue, you need to put this book down and go rewrite immediately.

Giving each character their own voice doesn't mean giving one a Boston accent and another a British accent. That's lazy writing. What it means is give each character their own inner voice which manifests in their dialogue.

Think about this: you know how some of your friends or co-workers are all of the same general race, gender, educational background, maybe even religious upbringing? Yet, none of them talk the same, none of them sound the same. Not just the timbre of their voices, but the *way* they speak. Their idiomatic phrasing, their favorite expressions, their verbal ticks. How the pitch of their voice changes depending on their mood or situation. That's how you need to write dialogue. Even characters related by blood shouldn't sound the same unless it's a story point.

The best course you can take on writing dialogue is being a good listener. I am always listening. To people I'm speaking with, and when I'm eavesdropping in public. The better listener you are, the better writer of dialogue you'll be. Whether you prefer your characters to speak in heightened methods ala Sorkin, or geographically and educationally specific methods like Scott Frank, listening is the best way to get better.

When I say listen to how people speak, that doesn't mean simply copying what they say or how they say things. Sometimes that's great. I have absolutely taken a line or speech pattern I heard and written it exactly as my ear caught it. But being a good listener also means running what you hear through the filter of your own writer's Voice. You will be amazed at how quickly your dialogue writing improves.

I'm doing my best to help you here with something that really can't be taught. I've read several different gurus' takes on how to write great dialogue and other than the mention of listening to conversations, the rest of their advice is awful. You'll hear them say good dialogue is about expressing some story point or good dialogue is about advancing the plot. No, that's called bad dialogue. Don't believe me? Go read a script by Sorkin or Tarantino or whatever writer you love and see how much great dialogue has zero to do with plot advancement.

Because dialogue isn't math.

Good dialogue is about people. Characters. Relationships.

My favorite quote on writing—and I've read thousands—comes from Tony Gilroy, and I don't believe a truer statement has ever been made regarding my profession . . .

"The quality of your writing is absolutely capped at your understanding of human behavior. You will never write above what you know about people."

If you don't understand what this means, I must be brutally honest and say, you have a long road ahead of you before you begin to nurture any talent as a screenwriter.

My writing absolutely leveled up the more I understood human behavior. I was a train wreck of a human for a long time, and it wasn't until I became self-aware that I could finally understand human behavior. I'm not sure one can understand human behavior on any decent level until one understands themselves. Self-awareness is key to being a great screenwriter . . . QT notwithstanding.

Once I became truly self-aware, I could self-actualize. Self-actualization is very different from the much more common self-image actualization. A lot of people think they are self-actualizing when all they're really doing is projecting an *image* of themselves they hope will impress others.

The better I know myself, the better I know other people. We view everyone through our own prisms, and if those prisms are fogged or cracked or broken, the view isn't quite as accurate.

Understanding human behavior is a huge asset in writing good dialogue.

That's all I have for you.

9

WHY YOUR PROFESSOR WON'T RECOMMEND *KILL THE DOG*

SCREENWRITING CANNOT BE TAUGHT . . . *it can only be learned.*

My publisher was rather uncomfortable with this section. When a book is recommended or (even better) made required reading in a college or university curriculum, it can boost sales. But whether this book sells one copy (thanks, Josh!) or one million, I'm going to remain committed to the truth.

I've always been interested in giving back. I do few things well, but screenwriting is one of them. I also play golf decently, make a quality Old Fashioned, and climb hills on my bike pretty well for someone of my less-than-ideal fitness level. But I digress.

Here's the problem with most all of academia regarding screenwriting: It's ALL analysis after the fact. While this works when one is teaching economics or biology, it fails when it comes to screenwriting. This is the same reason so many of the How-To books fail. It is all forensics analysis after the fact.

Professors and authors of How-To books love to break down, reverse-engineer, and analyze movies and television episodes, pointing out the different formulas and what they mistakenly call structure . . .

See? Here's the Hero's Journey. See? Here's Snyder's Beats.

If you research the professors who are teaching screenwriting across the United States (and I have), you will see that less than 10% of them have any genuine experience as professional screenwriters. But most all hold various academic honors. They love to wave their MFAs and PhDs like some battlefield flag as proof they know of what they speak. Unfortunately, no academic degree of any sort has anything to do with whether one knows how to write screenplays, let alone teach how to write them.

Some of these professors might have experience in the sense of . . . perhaps their 11-minute opus from a dozen years ago won the "Smilingest Audience" Award at the Roanoke Rapids Short Film Festival and Bake Sale. Or they once worked in some capacity at some entity that was connected in some way to another entity that worked with a company that was involved in some project that had Jimmy Fallon in it, so the professor's bio will read, "*Worked with Jimmy Fallon!*" Or maybe their documentary on the mating habits of the scarlet honeycreeper was raved about at the county library screening. Sometimes you'll see their bios list something akin to, "*Their screenplay* A SCARLET HONEYCREEPER'S REGRETS, *based on their own documentary, was optioned by Carl's Movie Studio & Carwash.*"

Despite a master's or doctorate in any number of subjects, they have no real-world experience in the art and craft of professional screenwriting.

> You are not entitled to your opinion. You are only entitled to your informed opinion.
>
> HARLAN ELLISON

Before anyone blows a gasket, let me state for the record I give mad props to people with higher learning degrees of any sort. It shows commitment, dedication, and patience. And I love teachers. I LOVE them. A good teacher is arguably as important as a good parent in a person's life. Teachers are some of the most underpaid and underappreciated folks on the planet, and most definitely in the United States. If it weren't for a couple of teachers I had in high school, there's a solid chance I'd be in prison now, or worse. I'm not kidding.

Back to screenwriting professors . . .

A master's degree is awarded upon completion of a course of study demonstrating mastery of a high-order overview of a specific field of study. It means the person possesses an advanced knowledge of theoretical and applied topics, and advanced skills in critical analysis.

You know what that last part means in our context? They have advanced skills in analyzing finished films, and (if you're lucky) finished scripts. They have no advanced skills in screenwriting.

Perhaps some holders of a master's will nit-pick my definition, but my point is every word in the above paragraph has zero to do with what it takes to create from the blank page. When it comes to the actual art and craft of what we do, I will bet all my NCIS residuals that a person whose higher learning ceased at a high school GED but has been writing screenplays for the last ten years knows more about what it takes to do it well than a person who has spent those same ten years in academia analyzing, studying, and dissecting how others do it.

Screenwriting cannot be taught. It can only be learned.

This doesn't mean the folks with their degrees aren't lovely, caring human beings who *think* they're serving you the best way possible. The problem is their deeply held opinions on how to properly do it are formed from the same place the gurus form their opinions—forensic analysis after the fact.

They break down scripts (or more often, finished films) into pieces, then fit all the pieces back together telling you this is how the writer did it.

Only that is unquestionably not how the writer did it.

The most egregious action I see is when these academics claim they know the best way to write a screenplay because despite having never written one themselves (or worse, written bad ones) they have broken down, analyzed, and written dissertations on the finished product of more motion pictures than a math professor can count.

Now, you can learn a lot from this way of teaching if you want to major in something like film history. You can also learn things about editing, and how certain aspects of filmmaking influence other aspects: sound, color, costume, cinematography, composition. But you cannot learn anything that helps you create a screenplay from the blank page.

When I hear academics trumpeting the benefits of forensic analysis of finished films and episodes of television, it tells me immediately they are clueless about how Hollywood really works. Because, apart from perhaps a couple of Clint Eastwood directed films, there is almost no film in cinematic history which made it to the screen looking exactly like the writer's screenplay.

Directors, actors, producers, cinematographers, editors, music people, stunt performers, budgets, weather, teamsters, and another hundred or so entities and situations all bring changes (good and awful) to the final product which the writer often has no control over or input on. When a professor breaks down a screenplay based on a finished motion picture, they are leading you down a path rife with unforeseen obstacles and dangers which can do more harm than good.

It's unfortunately quite common for a supercilious professor to express deprecation (or passion) for exactly what a writer was *doing* or *thinking* with a particular scene or script. They will talk ad nauseam about how CASABLANCA, CHINATOWN, THE SILENCE OF THE LAMBS, <INSERT VENERABLE TITLE HERE>, is a perfect screenplay because the screenwriter diligently followed all the Cat Saving, Hero's Journeying, Beat Sheeting, 22-sequencing, Story Circling steps necessary to write a great script.

However, the reality is that said scene or script was at best a result of a collaboration between the writer and many other non-writing entities, or at worst, something the writer had absolutely nothing to do with and wasn't even aware of until seeing the finished product. There's a reason the WGA had to put it into our MBA with the studios the screenwriter of a film is *invited* to the premiere of the movie that would not exist if the writer hadn't first created it! Yes, Hollywood was so convinced the writer has so little to do with a finished motion picture we had to force them to invite us to see the fruits of our own creations.

University professors love to discuss how a writer structured a script because it feeds right into the foundation of all academia: study, breaking down, and analyzing after the fact. They love to show some classic film and point out how the screenplay was so perfectly structured there was no way it could have been anything other than the amazing film it is. CHINATOWN might be a perfectly structured script, but it wasn't written that way. Don't believe me? Go watch any interview with Robert Towne about it.

What's funny is when you hear the professors dare to analyze BUTCH CASSIDY AND THE SUNDANCE KID, ROCKY, or some other rule-breaking film, they make all these excuses for it, always ending their didactic claims with the timeless, "*You have to know the rules to break the rules!*"

I'd rather have a root canal done by a one-eyed dentist wearing oven mitts than hear that silly apothegm ever again.

There are no rules. There is nothing to break.

A film that's super fun to mention to the professors and gurus is THE GODFATHER PART 2. A film (and screenplay) that is considered one of the greatest ever, arguably better than the first, but the experts rarely discuss it because they have no idea why it works so well. When they do the forensic analysis of that film looking for their beats and formulas and rules, and all their schematic models of success, it goes against everything they preach. That screenplay is a complete disaster when it comes to academia's rules of structure. And it's absolutely brilliant. Hmm.

I'm sure you'll hear all the uninformed experts explain away the success of the Oscar-winning screenplay EVERYTHING EVERYWHERE ALL AT ONCE with all sorts of verbal Jiu-Jitsu. I can hear their hammers right now as they pound away, trying to fit the round pegs of that script into their square forensic holes.

Do you really think it's just some random coincidence that what are considered the best screenplays ever written rarely if ever conform to these so-called rules of how to write screenplays?

Here's the craziest part of all this . . . the college and university professors achieve their fancy degrees in part by reading the books written by the gurus and charlatans we discussed in previous chapters. The authors of those books and their bad advice are then validated because professors promote the books as relevant, important contributions to learning the craft of screenwriting. It's a circle so vicious it would devour Harmon's Story Circle in one bite!

The professors and the books show you examples of incredibly successful finished films which they claim all follow the same rules, the same structure, etc. But what these folks never do is give you examples of terrible films that all followed those same rules and structure. Why don't they do this? Seems like it would be incredibly helpful, right? They don't do it because they don't know. They have no clue why one screenplay or film is great, and another one is terrible when both followed the same formulas/steps/rules/etc. Yet, the answer is so simple . . .

IT'S BECAUSE OF THE WRITING. Not the structure, not the plot points, not the finished product after directors, actors, sound, music, editors, etc., etc., etc., all put their fingerprints on it. What makes one screenplay better than another is the writing.

And that is why all the forensic analysis, all the breaking apart and putting back together does not help anyone write a better screenplay. Because what makes a screenplay good or great versus what makes one bland and unoriginal is what all the books and professors, and all their forensic analyses can't teach you:

Imagination. Whimsy. Inspiration. Emotion. Experience. Voice.

All the things that make one screenplay's writing stand out from all the others. Yet, one of the two most popular books ever published on screenwriting claims imagination will get you nowhere without knowing all the so-called rules said book imparts over its nearly 500 pages. Written by a person who desperately tried to be a successful screenwriter . . . and failed. Failed by writing the way his book (and all the others) claim you must write in order to not fail.

Screenwriting cannot be taught. It must be learned. You must be autodidactic. You can only learn it from life experience paired with writing and writing and writing. In your own Voice. In your own way. I believe the only way to achieve this is by being passionate about *being a writer* more than you are about the potential outcome or result.

You must love the act, the process, the actual doing of it more than you love the idea of outcome. You must truly love those awful days when nothing is working and you want to bang your head against the keyboard every bit as much as you love the days when you hit that rare flow state, and it's coming out of you faster than you can type. Okay, maybe not quite as much, but close.

One can analyze hundreds of films, read dozens of screenplays, devour all the How-To books, take all the screenwriting courses, listen to all the professors with their framed degrees, and still know nothing more about actual screenwriting than when they watched their very first film or read their very first script. Because the only way you learn is by doing. It is art. It is craft. It is not economics or biology. And while they will tell you they absolutely agree with the idea that one must write and write to become skilled at it, the problem is *the way* they teach you to write, which is what we've discussed ad nauseam . . . the tail wagging the dog.

Good screenplays should not be graded based on the way a finished film or television episode is broken down and analyzed.

But let me go on record here and say, it's not the professors' fault. Blame academia.

The very foundation of academia is research, study, analysis, and theory. It is consumed with making left-brain sense of creativity. Reducing the magic of creativity and imagination down to binary explanations.

Unfortunately, what academia tries to eliminate is the *very thing* creators need to provoke . . . mystery.

You must have written and written and written to understand this. What makes a screenwriter is screenwriting.

Academics can break down screenplays or films after the fact—it's what they do best—but they can't talk about *the process*. And that is why I believe all the screenwriting books out there, and all the screenwriting courses at colleges and universities, are hurting aspiring professionals more than helping. Because process is everything. And the most critical part of that process—arguably even more than discipline and commitment—is what I mentioned before . . . imagination. Whimsy. Inspiration. Voice.

Let's take ROCKY for example. Nearly fifty years later, it's still a screenplay held up by all the professors and gurus as perfection, and a script that spawned one of the most successful franchises in cinematic history. Yet, when you do the forensic analysis, you see how it completely fails when it comes to following the rules of the books and professors. Some of the books explain away this phenomenon by saying the silly "*it breaks the rules!*" garbage, or it "*messes with structure*." My eyes are rolling as I type that. What's worse is some books actually acknowledge the fact Stallone's script does not follow their rules, yet still insist you must follow their rules if you want to succeed!

When Sylvester Stallone wrote ROCKY, he did it over a few days, and I will guarantee you he never once—not for one second during the writing of that script—ever thought about inciting incidents or midpoint turns, or what page number something must happen on, or any of the other forensic after the fact junk.

He just wrote from his heart.

As a result, that script has its inciting incident not within the first 10–15 pages as you've been told MUST happen, but rather at the bottom of page . . . wait for it . . .

Page 53. Of a 115-page script. How many professors or gurus would tell you it's perfectly fine to write a script where the inciting incident happens halfway through the story?

Stallone wrote a compelling, entertaining story with a beginning, middle, and end. He gave us 50some pages to fall in love with the characters, to elicit an emotional response from the reader, before we ever get to the big plot point/inciting incident.

He wrote what he KNEW. Characters he knew. Characters he cared about and was invested in. He wrote in his own Voice. And that's why we, the readers and viewers, care about and are invested in that story.

Imagine if Stallone had taken a university screenwriting class before writing his script. None of us would have ever heard of ROCKY or its offspring, and Sly would probably be living in a 6th-floor walkup and telling the sketchy dude in 4B about his time on the set of THE PARTY AT KITTY AND STUD'S.

If you want a more contemporary example, how about Zach Cregger's 2022 breakout hit BARBARIAN? Another screenplay the experts say "turns structure on its head!" Really? So, there's no beginning, middle, or end? I must've seen a different film and read a different script. Zach has said in multiple interviews that he loves the Viverrine rescue job. He admitted he's even written scripts trying to do exactly what the book says to do on exactly what page. Guess what? Those scripts didn't sell. Yet, when he wrote BARBARIAN, he completely abandoned the kitty litter fodder and all the other professional instruction and simply wrote the story he wanted to write in his own Voice, his own way. What happened? He created a screenplay that has likely launched a very successful Hollywood career.

I'll end this with two points . . .

1. I don't have anything against professors of screenwriting. I know many. Some are definitely arrogant and bitter, and some are truly wonderful people who genuinely care. They simply have an uninformed opinion on what it takes to become a good screenwriter.

2. Ray Bradbury, widely considered one of our greatest scribes, said the following about academics when it comes to writing: "*I don't believe in college for writers. The thing is very dangerous. I believe too many professors are too opinionated and too snobbish and too intellectual, and the intellect is a great danger to creativity—because you begin to rationalize and make up reasons for things, instead of staying with your own basic truth—who you are, what you are, what you want to be. I've had a sign over my typewriter for 25 years which reads, "Don't think!" You must never think at the typewriter, you must feel.*"

Professors and courses cannot teach feel.

10

WRITER'S BLOCK

11

THE SCREENWRITER'S PROCESS

NOW THAT WE'VE gone through all the things not to do and all the folks not to listen to, I'm sure there's a decent number of you wondering, "*Okay, so then what DO I do?*"

Fear not, young Jedi. We're all in this together.

I don't mean that flippantly, or condescendingly. It is genuine. Writers need writers. Writing is one of the most solitary endeavors there is—that's why I've always preferred writing television to features. There are few environments in life that are as joyful, safe, hilarious, educating, and entertaining as a professional writers room. A healthy, inclusive, nontoxic writers room, I should say.

A good room run by a quality showrunner is simply one of the best things a writer can experience. A toxic room run by a bad showrunner is the exact opposite. It is a life-sucking, miserable experience where days feel like weeks, and weeks feel like years.

Whether you have been blessed enough to be part of a healthy writers room, or whether you are sitting alone working on your very first screenplay, we are all in this together. The writing community is one of the most supportive environments there is. Writers cheer for other writers.

Now, as I've mentioned there are no absolutes. Every working professional screenwriter, including myself, has heard the stories of insecure, paranoid writers consumed with jealousy of another writer. For whatever reason this seems much more common in the television comedy world than in dramas or features. My best advice to avoid falling into the trap of letting someone else's success bring you down is . . . don't read the Trades. It takes you five minutes to read them, and five days to get over them. If you're a veteran screenwriter currently in between gigs, and you read about some kid with no experience selling a spec script for seven figures, or some writer you mentored back in the day just got a two-season order and hired everyone except you, it can lead to . . . well, it's why therapists in Hollywood will never be out of work.

Bottom line is if you have any sort of self-esteem issues, stay away from the Trades. Most of what's in them is planted, anyway.

In all seriousness, most of my fellow working professional screenwriters want all of us to succeed. Just as writing begets writing, writers' success begets writers' success.

We're all in this together.

So, how do you apply all this newfound truth you're reading? The answer, the truthful answer is . . .

There is no answer.

Wait, don't throw the book across the room, or shut down your audio device. At least not yet.

There is no answer in the sense there is no definitive answer that works for every screenwriter.

One of the sheer joys of this gig is that it is so individualized, so unique to each one of us. How we write, where, our structuring (verb and noun), if we listen to music or nature sounds, or must write in complete silence, every part of the process is unique to each writer. What works for me may not work for you. What works for Malcolm Spellman may not work for Taika Waititi. What works for Bong Joon-Ho may not work for Greta Gerwig, and so on.

That said, whatever works FOR YOU is what will give you the best chance of success. Not trying to write like someone else.

What follows is simply my process. The way I do it. That is all it is. My own writing process developed and evolved over years of doing this professionally.

This is literally How I Write.

You may take some things from it that will help you be a more productive and better screenwriter. Or you may find none of it worth the time it took to read this chapter.

I've been writing stories since I was in 5th grade. I've been writing screenplays since I was in college. I've been getting paid to write screenplays for twenty-five years.

I'm better now than I was five years ago, much better than I was ten or twenty years ago, and compared to the completely lost kid I was when I arrived in Hollywood with my scripts handwritten in spiral notebooks . . . I'm not even close to the same writer.

Hold up. That's not completely accurate. The writer DNA that was in me from childhood, the imagination and love of story that carried me through my dark adolescence and school days, the desire and drive to create; to write movies and TV shows, still exists to this day.

What is different is my understanding of how to do it more effectively, more enjoyably, and more creatively. It is not that I know *the math* any better, but rather, the opposite of that. I know myself better, I understand human behavior better, and I trust myself. Even when I feel like a total fraud, which is the most important time to trust oneself.

My ability with language, with turns of phrase, and my vocabulary, have all evolved and advanced. The fact I know the difference between an acronym and an initialism. The fact I know "impactful" has only become a word today because of society's laziness and failure to use the proper word, "impactive."

The discovery of my Voice, the ability to process and use my life experiences—the importance of which cannot be measured—all of this makes me the writer I am at this moment. And mostly, cuz I've written a lot. A lot.

I keep working at it, not for money, but because I love it. I have often said whether I'm eating Top Ramen or at Nobu, I would be a writer. It's not about the money. I know folks scraping to get by hate hearing that. But it's true. Has the money been nice? Absolutely. I work in the single most overpaid industry on the planet. I thank God for this blessing every day. I have enjoyed what being overpaid has allowed me to do. Just look at my watch collection. But I state on the lives of my three precious children, if I never made another penny from writing, I would continue to write.

I have a tremendous passion for it and am driven to be the very best writer I can be. My passion isn't in the outcome or possible financial windfall. It is in the process.

I am a writer.

If you ever hear a professional writer say, "*I hate writing*," you have my permission to slap them. They're lying. If they truly hated it, they would do something else. There are many things much easier with the promise of greater financial security than writing. Dorothy Parker famously quipped, "I hate to write, but I love having written." Ever since she said that, writers have borrowed and tweaked this pithy statement in an effort to be as cool as Parker. No one can be as cool as Dorothy Parker. But many writers love to tell you how they hate writing. Again, not true. What they hate is perhaps the business side of being a professional writer (it can be evil), or they hate how hard they must work to write well because—pay attention here—writing is much more difficult for those who are good at it than it is for those who aren't. The Nobel Prize laureate, Thomas Mann, said, "*A writer is someone for whom writing is more difficult than it is for other people.*"

I love writing even when it's hard, even when it drains me mentally and emotionally. I love writing on the days when it flows and feels completely fluid and free. Those days are rare, and I begin each writing day with the hope of the Flow State.

As for my process, I will walk you through how it goes from the moment I get an idea through the first draft to the rewrite, to when it's finally DONE.

WHERE DO YOU GET YOUR IDEAS?

The question has been asked of writers so often it is now a cliché as old as <insert really old cliché here>. There is a slew of joke responses writers have come up with to answer this question. Some writers claim being asked this question enrages them.

Why does such a seemingly innocent and rational question spark so much umbrage among professional writers?

Because we don't know the answer. Imagine being an accountant or computer programmer, and you don't know the answer to the most basic question about what you do. How would you feel? Then imagine being asked that same question every time someone learns what you do for a living.

I understand the aversion to the question because it brings up feelings of frustration and fear. Frustration because we don't know the answer, and fear that if we think about it too much the ideas will stop coming.

My ideas come from my muse—a large black Newfoundland dog who speaks with a bit of a Cardiff accent. I never know when he'll show or how long he'll stay. He's generally friendly and supportive but can be impatient and condescending at times.

That's my fun answer. The real answer is my ideas come from everywhere and anywhere, and I never consciously go hunting for them.

I've had ideas for feature scripts and even entire television series come from things as seemingly insignificant as watching a person eating in a restaurant.

I came up with an idea for an episode of a series I was working on from watching BEAR IN THE BIG BLUE HOUSE with my (then toddler) daughter. I wrote a spec pilot which was never made, but developed a couple of times, from an idea I got from a single character in a thirty-five-year-old Hong Kong movie.

The television series pitch I sold in a bidding war was born out of a lunch with a crotchety old former newspaper reporter.

I've been in the middle of writing scripts—both on spec and under contract—when seeing something, hearing something, or remembering something opened creative floodgates and completely changed the direction of the script.

The bottom line is the ideas are always coming. I can't stop them. No writer can. We get so many ideas there's no way we could ever write them all. We are inherently observers—of life and human behavior. This is why we usually roll our eyes when someone tells us *they* have a great idea and just need us to write it. We're not rolling our eyes at the person (okay, sometimes we are), we are rolling our eyes because if the person only knew how many of our own ideas we already have, they'd never ask.

I'm going to take you through two different scripts I wrote. One was an episode for NCIS: NEW ORLEANS, and the other is a feature script I finished recently. You will see my process, including my quirks and idiosyncrasies, my doubts and fears, and how I take the very seed of an idea and see it through to a finished script.

The feature literally took years from my first thought of *"There's a movie here!"* to the final FADE OUT. That's not always the case. Some ideas go from inception to completion in a matter of weeks. Every idea and execution are different.

Regardless of what the idea is I'm working on, my process is the same:

CLOCKING IN

My writing days all begin the same way. It's the way I've done it since I was first exposed to this concept six or seven years ago. One of my all-time favorite films is Steve Zaillian's SEARCHING FOR BOBBY FISCHER, based on the true story of Josh Waitzkin, who was one of the youngest chess grandmasters in history. After his chess career, Josh became a world champion in Tai Chi. How many people do you know become the BEST in the world at two completely different things? Amazing. Josh is a hero of mine.

The way I begin my writing day came from him. You know how when you first wake up you immediately check your phone? Check email, social media, texts, whatever. Well, what happens when we do that is we are putting our brains immediately into a reactive state. The first thing we're doing after a night of restful sleep and recharging is reacting to outside stimuli. When you do this, you're putting the creative parts of your brain—the proactive states—behind the proverbial 8 ball. It just makes it much more difficult for your brain to get into the proactive state it needs to be in for the creative process.

What I learned from Josh was this . . . for the first 90 minutes of the day, I don't touch my phone. I don't check email, don't go on the internet, don't look at any texts. I don't look at anything on my phone but the time. That way, when I sit down to write, my brain is in the best proactive state it can be, and thus, operating at maximum focus and creativity.

This has been a game changer for me.

Sometimes I'll go three hours before I think to check my phone. But I never go less than 90 minutes. That's the absolute minimum. And I can attest to my creativity and productivity being exponentially increased by doing this. The thing is, it's not easy. It took me a good two weeks to form the habit. I was not able to just wake up one day and change a habit I had ingrained in myself for over a decade. But try it. You'll likely start and stop the first week or so, but once you fully commit to it, your creativity will level up.

SWITCH THE FIELD

I'm a big soccer fan, so big, I often refer to it by its proper name, football, which drives most of my American non-soccer friends a little nuts. But come on, America stole the name. And American Football should be called HANDBALL since they use their hands much more than they do their feet. And the handball folks won't mind. They seem like decent peeps.

But I digress.

I mention *futbol* because there's a term used in the game: switch the field. It means if you are attacking with the ball up one side of the pitch (the field), you can sometimes improve your chance of scoring by switching the field—moving the attack to the other side. It's also known as "Change the point" as in change the point of attack. Defenders can also switch the field, but this isn't a soccer book, so we won't go there.

In my writing process, I will often employ switching the field. Changing the point of attack. If I'm writing in my home office (where I do much of my work) and things aren't going well creatively, I will move. I will go to one of my favorite coffee houses, or if I really need a jolt of energy, I'll go to a hotel. I will change the point of attack.

By the way, I love writing in hotels. I am a morning writer, and at my best from 6am to about 10, so sometimes I will head to a hotel with a nice lobby area or quality restaurant and work there. On multiple occasions when I've been writing something particularly important or daunting, I check myself into a hotel for a few nights. I move in and rearrange the furniture in the room to suit my personal feng shui. The Peninsula in Beverly Hills and the Intercontinental in DTLA are so used to my behavior they'll make a comment when I check in . . . "*Welcome back, Mr. Guyot, are we here for pleasure or for some redecorating?*"

Your writing environment can have a massive impact on your writing process. I am a firm believer in your office is anywhere. The stories of writers like Stephen King and Sue Grafton and others writing their early work on folding chairs in their laundry rooms with their typewriters (look up what those are, kids) balanced on their thighs are legendary. You can and should be able to write anywhere. That said, I know from experience that switching up where you write can infuse new and positive energy into the process. I don't switch the field just to do it. I do it when I'm feeling the need for something fresh, some new bit of inspiration that isn't happening wherever I am.

The other time I change the point is when I'm working on multiple projects at once. I've become a very disciplined writer which means I'm up early six days a week and typing away. Some days I'm done before lunch. Other days I'm still writing as the sun sets. I don't force it. I've learned the hard way that isn't conducive to my creativity. For whatever reason I don't write well at night.

When I'm working on multiple projects, I break my writing into specific sections. Say, I'm writing a spec feature for myself while at the same time I'm under contract to write a television pilot. The contract gig obviously has priority. But there have been times recently where I was under contract on multiple projects at once. I break up those sections by days. An example of this would be:

Monday through Wednesday I work on project A. Thursday through Saturday, project B. I do it this way to avoid switching projects within the same day. However, sometimes that's necessary, and this is when I will switch the field. I will begin my morning working on project A, then at some point stop. I close the laptop and will literally restart my day. I might shower (even if I did earlier), I will change clothes, and I will work on the second project in a new space. If I began my day writing project A in my home office, I'll go to a hotel or coffee house for project B. Or vice-versa.

I do this to clear my head of any patina from the first project. I want complete focus and creativity on the second project. I create playlists for each project I write, and I will begin listening to project B's playlist as I'm driving to the coffee house or showering and putting on fresh clothes at home. This might sound like insanity, but this is what works for my process. And works well.

What follows is the story of how I came to write a spec feature we will call THE HEIST SCRIPT. I completed the latest draft a few months ago, and as of this writing, the script is with a major financing entity, and I hope you'll see it in theaters one day.

THE INCEPTION POINT

I was working as a Co-Producer on the CBS series JUDGING AMY, and the next episode I was to write introduced a new character who might become a series regular. The showrunner—the amazing Barbara Hall—had given me her concept and thoughts about who she wanted this character to be. It was up to me to figure out how to manifest that onto the page.

The character struggled in his personal life, and to contrast that, I thought I'd make him very precision oriented in his professional life. A small way I could show this was to have him wear a precision mechanical watch.

At the time, I knew nothing about watches, so I began one of the most satisfying parts of the job: research.

Let me interrupt myself to give you a mini-lesson on better screenwriting. As mentioned in the chapter on Voice, specificity is good. No matter what you might hear to the contrary, be specific when you can.

Don't write:

```
She looks at her expensive watch.
```

When you can write:

```
She glances at her Zenith Defy Lab; a watch as
tightly wound as she is.
```

Okay, back to my process.

I began to research mechanical watches, which means watches that don't run on batteries (Quartz). What should have been a ten-minute research dive was still going three days later, and eventually became a personal obsession of mine. I was so deep into the world of fine, high-end watches you would have needed a Trieste submarine to find me. I had become completely consumed by the world of mechanical watches. Truly fell in love with them. I contacted a man who ran a horological website and it turned out he happened to live in LA. He agreed to show me the secret world of expensive watches. *There's a secret world???* This was getting better by the second!

By the time I got back to writing my episode, I had completely forgotten my whole watch dive had been to give the character a watch. I wrote my episode and don't think the word watch was anywhere in it. Once free from my writing responsibilities, I was off to meet with the watch sage whom I will call Mr. Lew.

We met at a cafe in Beverly Hills and spent an hour discussing my job and his passion for watches and watch collecting. I got the sense Mr. Lew was vetting me in some way. He seemed to become more relaxed and comfortable the more we spoke, and by the end of our meal, he asked me if I wanted him to show me around the watch world of Beverly Hills.

Duh.

He walked me around all the luxury watch dealers, Vacheron Constantin, Jaeger-LeCoultre, Audemars Piguet, and the rest, giving me a history lesson on each manufacturer and their particular aesthetics and business practices. At the time, I was like everyone else and thought Rolex was the pinnacle of luxury watches. They aren't even halfway up the mountain.

Mr. Lew seemed to know every person we encountered in the watch boutiques. We viewed some of the most expensive watches in the world. He talked to me about the history of watchmaking, and what separates an exquisite $100,000 watch from a $2,000 piece. He told me about authorized dealers vs retailers and all sorts of insider knowledge on the business of selling high-end watches.

He explained there's a black market for everything in the world, including expensive watches. The black market for watches is the same as it is for anything else—a place you want to stay away from. Then he said there is a gray market, which isn't anything illegal per se, but rather a way around the high prices charged by ADs (authorized dealers) and retailers. In the gray market, you can find ADs (or collectors) who might be selling brand-new authentic timepieces for 20% off retail.

Then he asked me if I wanted to see the *dark* gray market.

The what?

This is where the highest of the high-priced pieces are sold and traded at very substantial discounts, far more than the gray's 20%. The timepieces aren't stolen, aren't damaged, they are perfect. But there's a whole thing I won't go into here (because this is a screenwriting book) about the watch industry's insider war between manufacturers, ADs, retailers, and watch collectors. Part of the battle is manufacturers often release new pieces in very limited quantities with great fanfare, and potential customers go crazy trying to get their hands on them, doing whatever they can to get on the notorious waitlists, and often paying as much as 200% ABOVE retail.

Enter the dark gray market.

As Mr. Lew and I turned into what looked like just another Beverly Hills jewelry store, he greeted the person behind the counter with great familiarity. The person buzzed us through a gate to the space behind the counter.

I followed Mr. Lew through a curtain into the backroom of the store. We nodded at two people working on jewelry as we passed. At the end of the backroom, a door led down a narrow staircase. We descended into a concrete passageway, and I realized we were under Beverly Hills.

We walked for at least a hundred yards before we came to another staircase that led up to another backroom that was probably half the size of the first one.

To this day I have no idea where this backroom is, what business it was part of, nothing. I never saw anything but the space, which was concrete walls lined with metal shelves containing plastic containers of various sizes.

In the corner of the room was a small desk with all sorts of jeweler's equipment on it. A large, Eastern European man in his 50s sat behind the desk looking through a loupe at a platinum watch in his hand. He greeted Mr. Lew with familiarity but was very concerned about who I was. Lew assured him of my bona fides, explaining I was a screenwriter, and he was "teaching" me about the world of horology. The man relaxed. A little.

After some quiet discussion between the two, Euro guy pulled a green container off a shelf that held a few innocuous cardboard boxes.

Mr. Lew explained to me I was about to see a certain manufacturer's newest limited-edition piece—only 20 of them were created—which were selling in boutiques for over $150,000 IF you could get on the waitlist to purchase one.

Of the twenty that existed in the world, two of them were inside this dank backroom hidden under Beverly Hills. The watches were stunning. Mr. Lew informed me I could purchase one of these two for $78,000, a fraction of the retail price.

At this point, my mind had gone from being a newbie watch lover back to a screenwriter. I KNEW there was a movie in all this. Secret staircases? Backrooms with mysterious men? Rare timepieces sitting in cardboard boxes? Are you kidding me???

Over the next few weeks, I couldn't get that Beverly Hills experience out of my mind. I had no clue what the movie was, I just knew I had seen a world that very few people on the planet knew existed.

As I finished out that season on JUDGING AMY, I was married with two very young kids, and my then-wife and I decided to move away from LA to raise our family. We moved to her hometown of Saint Louis, Missouri, and I assumed I would maybe teach, or write novels for a living, all while typing away on spec scripts. The good Lord had other plans.

We hadn't even closed on our house when I was hired to write and produce a pilot for Stephen J. Cannell. That took up most of my bandwidth for the next year and led to another pilot the following year, then an overall deal at a studio. I was suddenly more in demand as a television writer than I had ever been while living in LA.

As I was busy writing pilots that weren't getting ordered to series, I never forgot about that watch world idea, but I wasn't giving it any energy or thought. It just sat in the very back of my mind over the next year or so. Then in 2007, I went to see OCEAN'S 13, the second sequel to one of my favorite films of all time, the 2001 OCEAN'S ELEVEN remake.

Sitting in the middle of a dark theater watching 13, my watch movie idea exploded back into my mind.

A heist! A WATCH HEIST! Something I'd never seen on screen!

I could barely focus on the last thirty minutes of the film because my writer's mind was vibrating like the movement inside a Mikrogirder (that was for my watch peeps).

Over the next few weeks, I went about my life working on television projects, being a father, and just *thinking* about the idea. The movie slowly began to come into focus for me. The first images were of it being a darker film along the lines of RONIN or THIEF (my favorite Michael Mann flick). What with the secret passages and scary European men, what else could it be? So, someone is stealing watches. But who's stealing them? And more importantly WHY?

At this point, all I had was a heist idea with watches as the MacGuffin. Also, and this is important to my process, I had yet to write anything down. This was all just swirling around in my head. Day after day, week after week. Tony Gilroy describes this part of the process as, "*Walking around the city with a secret.*"

I needed a main character. Or two. For me, no matter how cool or commercial an idea or "plot" is, everything begins and ends with character. I believe plot does not exist without character. I knew I needed a character as fantastic as Ted Griffin's Danny Ocean or Michael Mann's Frank if this was going to be a great screenplay. Clooney as Danny Ocean is about as perfect casting as there's ever been, but the character was on the page before a foot of film was shot.

As the idea floated around my brain, OCEAN'S ELEVEN became my True North. I was moving away from a Michael Mann tone, and more toward Ted Griffin. This wasn't something I was doing consciously, it was just happening. I was beginning to see other characters popping into the story. Probably because one of my favorite tropes of heist films is the assembling of the crew.

For my protagonist, I obviously didn't want to do some derivative version of Danny Ocean or anyone else, but I was definitely thinking about characters from other films who had moved me on an emotional level. I think sometimes newer writers feel they aren't allowed to draw from previous work. Like it's some form of plagiarism. Inspiration is not the same as straight up IP theft. So long as you're not just rewriting someone else's characters or script, you're fine to think about other writers' work for inspiration.

PHASE 1: *SKETCHING*

At this point, it became time to put pencil to paper. I have this wonderful leather-bound traveler's notebook from a tiny shop in Altadena, California called Baum-Kuchen. Every single writing project of mine starts in this book. Don't ask me why, but I always begin writing by hand. I always use Palomino Blackwing pencils and always write in my traveler's notebook.

The very first words I put down were just simple thoughts about characters from other films to drawn upon.

Here are the first three lines I wrote for the heist script all those years ago:

> ***Tone = Italian Job? O11?***
> ***De Niro—RONIN.***
> ***Theron—Italian Job.***

Other than the tone I thought I wanted all I was thinking about beyond stealing watches was character. Nothing about loglines or inciting incidents or plot machinations. Just character. Since I had no characters for my world yet, I thought about a couple of great ones from other heist films: De Niro's Sam in RONIN, and Charlize Theron's Stella from the ITALIAN JOB remake. I wasn't thinking about a male and female character yet, I was just waiting for my muse to show up with my protagonist. This is the unteachable stuff. I didn't know yet if my protagonist would be a man or a woman. All I was thinking about were characters I liked seeing on screen or reading in scripts. I don't know why I wrote these two down. I guess the Theron movie had just come out not too long before, and I was a big fan of RONIN.

My next move was to begin watching heist films. I wanted to immerse myself in the world of heist stories. Some writers avoid watching anything similar to what they're working on, but for me, I need all the help I can get, and the more I'm *inside* the world I want to write in, the better my creative mind works. Over the next several months I think I watched around thirty heist films, from THE KILLING to LE CERCLE ROUGE to THE STING to NO BLOOD NO TEARS to FLAWLESS. Some I watched two and three times.

I wasn't looking for any tropes or scenes to emulate or rip off, I was just putting myself in that storytelling mindset. I wanted everything I thought about to be colored in the world of heists. I would occasionally make notes about an action sequence or characterization—nothing more than just a line or two—something for me to use as inspiration down the road. I watched a great Korean film called THE THIEVES which contains some fantastic sequences. Nothing in my finished script is close to what's in this film, but just its tone and execution helped charge my own creative batteries.

As the idea simmered on low at the very back of my brain stove, my characters began to form. For whatever reason—I have no idea why—the name DANE popped into my head early on. I imagined another character calling this person "The Great Dane." Names are important to me, and I'll change characters' names several times throughout a project until I feel it's right for who they are. Dane was rare in that it remained from the beginning all the way through the last draft.

Now, I needed to figure out who Dane was. Who is driving this story? When the name hit, the gender hit. Dane was a man. I first imagined Denzel as Dane. I often cast my characters early on just to have a sense of who they are physically. I knew I wanted him to be someone with a deep passion for mechanical watches. But why would someone like that ever steal watches? The WHY was (and always is) a big part of my story construction. If the idea doesn't have a solid why for the characters at its core, it's not worth writing.

Maybe the story could be some sort of Robin Hood idea? Maybe he's stealing watches from someone who stole them first? That's a solid Why. Yes! He's the Good Thief! Stealing back from the bad thief. And this will be a great foundation for Dane's simple emotional journey.

All of this went into my notebook.

NOTE: I still didn't have a quality why. Dane's why. Why was he stealing back from the bad guy?

The next thing I did was look at any notes I had from the research with Mr. Lew. I looked back at the notes I had taken during those early days and transferred any I thought were worthwhile into my notebook. Any little kernel of information that might go into the screenplay. The way the light hit the face of the Euro guy. Any information on the history of the manufacturers, what giant conglomerates own what brands. Any technical information on movements. Whatever I thought might be something that could end up in the script.

ASIDE: Most of this stuff is nowhere to be seen in any drafts of the script, but it's all part of the DNA of every draft.

This part of my process I call sketching. I'm just *sketching*, playing around with thoughts, not committing to anything. Again, this isn't some trick I learned from someone, or some "rule" that must be adhered to, it's just how I've always done it.

I don't have any set amount of time or word count for my sketching phase. It can be days, weeks, or months. I just do it until I *feel* I'm ready to move into Phase 2.

PHASE 2: *THE WORD DOCUMENT*

Phase 2 is transferring all my sketching into some sort of coherent WORD document. I take all the notes I've written, all the bits of dialogue and character thoughts, the locations, or things I've seen or imagined, and create my first official document for the idea. I rarely have a title at this point, and I don't worry about it. Titles come. That's another place where the mouser liberation book goes seriously off the rails. You do NOT need a "killer title" and "killer logline" before you write. Not one of the Club WPS members

I've mentioned in these pages needs that before writing, so why would you?

The first document I created for this script was called "Watch-Heist-v1.0."

This document becomes much more official in the sense that at the top I have what amounts to a mission statement. I write what the movie is as I see it at this moment (which may not be much), and more importantly, I write down WHY I am writing it. Why I need to commit the time and energy to this story. The Why for this one was because I had been so moved emotionally by that day in Beverly Hills and because I had fallen so in love with mechanical watches and the world of collectors that I wanted to tell the story. It was a script I wanted to read. A movie I wanted to see.

Never at any time during this process did I think about things like, is this commercial, will this sell, what do I need to do to make sure people like it. None of that garbage. I was focused on creating something for myself.

Now here's the super cool thing, and this is what happens to writers. What I didn't know at the time is that the story I wanted to write was really about fathers and sons. About my relationship with my father. That's the core theme of the script. That's what I was truly writing about. That's the simple emotional journey. Not watches, not heists. But I would have never finished the thing let alone made it any good if I had begun by trying to write about fathers and sons. For me, it must happen organically. YMMV.

Some screenwriters start with theme. Others let the theme evolve. I'm in the latter camp. I rarely think about theme at any point before being deep into the writing of the script. For me, when I've tried to chase theme, it's never a good result. My brain isn't big enough to write clearly about some grand theme. I have to write my little character story, and then at some point go, *"Ohhhh, that's what I'm writing about."*

I highly recommend writing yourself a mission statement at the beginning of any project. It can really help to go back and look at it during times when you're creatively stuck or feel like you've lost your way.

After the mission statement, I make two new documents that I'll eventually blend with my original. One for characters, and one for something I label SWWS: Scenes We Want to See. These are anything from my handwritten notes that could be scenes. For a heist film, there are obviously the trope scenes, and though I didn't yet know what those scenes looked like, I knew I wanted them. In my SWWS document, I had:

- Assemble crew.
- Showcase the watches
- Big final heist.

Doesn't look like much, right? It's not. I'm not throwing fastballs yet; I'm just warming up.

Could I mix my metaphors any more in this book?

As I said, one of my favorite tropes in classic heist films is getting the crew together, usually back together. Since I love these scenes, I knew this part of the script would be important to me, and something I was going to have a lot of fun writing.

Before I could work on any of these scenes, though, I needed to know the characters, and most importantly, understand their relationships to each other. It's not characters that make the reader turn the pages of your screenplay, it's the characters' relationships with the other characters. You can have the coolest, most interesting character on paper, but if they have no one to relate to, no one to come up against, fall in love with, etc., you have nothing.

I wrote a bunch of versions of who Dane was and why he would steal watches. Eventually, I hit on the idea that the only reason a guy like this would do it is if it was personal. Deeply personal. The watches were stolen from him. No . . . from his family. His father. And it destroyed his father.

Once I felt like I had a grasp on that, I started to write up who his fellow thieves might be. I made sure to give each character their own POV and voice. What followed next was working on the characters' relationships with each other. I don't write extensive character backstories like some writers. But I do spend a lot of time and energy thinking about who they are, and how and why they're in the world of my story.

Only after I have my story's characters roughed out, and who they are to each other, do I turn my attention to the heist itself.

What watches are they stealing? How about the world's most expensive watches? Well, that's something that's amorphous. How about the world's most famous watches? Better. But would those be worth millions? How about watches that all have some vital connection to the history of watches and the industry of watchmaking? Hmm. Watches like that would definitely be expensive.

From there I do some research. What watches are considered the most important? This is where internet research can let you down, but more on that later.

I think about the collection of watches, where they would be, and how they would be stolen. Does the crew go to each individual watch and steal it? No, we don't want a four-hour movie. Okay, so all the watches are together in some collection, like in a museum or something. How many? Twenty is good. No, too many. Ten. Yes.

The MacGuffin is a collection of the ten most famous/important watches in history.

Back to research. The internet can be great for research, but it can also hurt you. There are some things where you must go beyond the Google machine and do actual, real-world research.

To know what watches would be in this collection I could not rely on my own opinion, or those of watch journalists on the internet, or silly Reddit rooms, or Quora discussions.

I went to the people. I connected with some people who lived and breathed the high-end world of timepieces all day, every day. These folks were from all over the world. I spoke with folks from New York to London to Singapore to Spain. And what I got from their generosity is the stuff Google CAN'T give you. The behind-the-scenes stories, the TRUTH. I realized it's just like Hollywood; no matter what you see or read on the internet, no matter how reliable the source, unless you have been on the set, or in the meetings, unless you have seen and heard it with your own eyes and ears, you don't know the truth.

I compiled so much great research from these folks it wouldn't all fit into my story, and thus, I began thinking about a sequel . . . not literally, but just enough that I made a note to add a single line at the end of the script to indicate this crew would likely do another heist.

So, now I had my ten watches. I had my protagonist. I had his crew. Who was my antagonist? I spent the next several days figuring that out.

You've all heard a hero is only as good as the villain, and all the variations on that. It's true. But you don't need to think in terms of "heroes and villains." Protagonist and antagonist is just fine. Your story doesn't have to have two characters battling with swords or guns or dragons. They can battle just as intensely with intellect and emotion.

Because this story was born out of my passion for watches, I knew the antagonist was going to be a dick. I mean, come on, who steals watches? Seriously, the way I went about creating my antag was by thinking about my protag. For me, the best antagonists are when they are . . . how do I say this . . . when the protagonist and antagonist are two sides of the same coin. That's compelling to me. So, my antagonist was created from the DNA of my protagonist.

Eventually, I had enough of the story in my head, the characters, the conflicts, and most importantly the ending, to start thinking about scenes and sequences.

Speaking of the end, part of my process is I always know the end of my story. Sometimes I will literally have the final scene visualized. But I always know the ending insofar as what it is emotionally for the characters. Again, this is by no means a requirement, it's just how I do it. By the time I get to beat sheets or outlines, I know how I want the story to open, and how it ends. Knowing the end gives me that True North I can write toward. For this script, I saw the final scene in my head and knew what the last line of dialogue was going to be.

Now, I was ready to beat out the story.

PHASE 3: BEAT SHEETS

My beat sheet phase is short. I create a document with maybe the four or five main beats of the script. This is literally what my first beat sheet contained:

1. **Opening—original heist**
2. **Dane gets second chance**
3. **Dane gets crew together**
4. **Plan heist**
5. **heist**
6. **Beach**

That's it. No details, nothing but those few words. I knew the final scene was set on a beach. That's why "beach." I knew I wanted the opening scene to be a heist that happened in the past. It was a great way to meet all the characters and get to know them and their relationships so when it's time to assemble them again, there's more emotional weight to the trope. And you get to show how competent they are at their job. Competence porn is something we all love. Everybody loves to see people who are really good at something, be it athletics, music or safecracking.

Also, note that my above beats don't adhere to any rules you've seen, or cat beats, etc. This is just how I do it. What works best for me. You may have a different way that works better for you. For me, the beats in a beat sheet are just signposts. I write from character. Character first and always. Yet, when I beat out a story, and even in the outline phase, most of what those documents focus on is the external stuff. I might drop internal thoughts and character things into my outlines, but I save the heavy lifting of character for the actual writing of the script. I have my map of where I want my story to go, and then I fill the negative space which is most critical during the actual writing.

From here I will do perhaps another beat sheet or two, but they never contain more than eight or ten beats at most. Any more than that and it's an outline. The reason I do this seemingly innocuous phase is to warm up slowly. I've learned the hard way that trying to force ideas and rush the process is death. I don't want to put any pressure on myself. Pressure is the evil antagonist of creativity.

Once I feel like I'm ready to fill in more negative space between beats, I go to outline.

I hate outlining. Outlining sucks. But I will not write anything without outlining first.

There's a misconception with outlining. People think if you outline a story then you are locked into telling that story that way and cannot deviate from it. When I hear writers talk about how they don't outline because they don't want to be "locked in" to a certain path or story, I know they really don't understand outlining.

Think of an outline as a map or GPS. You want to drive from Portland, Oregon to Miami, Florida. You have a map to tell you how to get there. It is completely up to you whether you follow the map's suggestion for the best way to get there. You can follow the map succinctly, or you can start out heading south or east, go see Bryce Canyon in Utah, stop for a bite at Eskimo Joe's in Stillwater, check out the Rhubarb capital of Illinois, grab a selfie by the world's largest fire hydrant in South Carolina, and still find your way down to Miami because YOU HAVE A MAP. You can get back on point whenever you choose.

When you don't have a map and just start heading south, you will eventually get to Miami if you're lucky, but it will take you longer and more importantly, the trip won't be as enjoyable.

I have a good friend who writes bestselling novels—yes, I know, every author calls themselves a bestseller, but Lee really is one—and he loves to say how he never outlines a thing; he just sits down and starts writing. This works for prose writers much better than it does for screenwriters because part of the entire prose journey is eating at Eskimo Joe's and taking selfies by the big fire hydrant. For screenwriters, due to the nature of the beast, we are writing within a certain degree of confinement compared to prose writers, and for the most part, we are all on the clock. But that hasn't stopped some of you from trying to write a screenplay without outlining, right? How did that go?

I outline because screenwriting is hard. And I'm not a good enough writer to just start typing without anything more than an idea. My outline phase is a concentric circle. However, there is one critical part of my process that happens between the beat sheets and outlines, and I am incapable of writing anything without this phase . . .

PHASE 4: *THE PLAYLIST*

I don't know when it started, or why. I just know I cannot write anything without first creating a playlist. Back in the pre-Spotify days, I had over 6000 songs in my iTunes. I love music. I love many different forms and styles of music. And for whatever reason I can't write any sort of story until I have the "soundtrack" in my head.

As I'm building the world of my story, from inception point through research and notes and sketching and beat sheets, what is happening inside my mind is I am finding the rhythm and tone of the piece.

For the heist script, it was very much a jazzy tone. If you think back to the music of OCEAN'S ELEVEN, it was a similar vibe. I knew my heist script needed this type of rhythm, this tone.

Looking back at my playlist for this script, it's two hours and forty-two minutes, and here are just a few of the tunes on it:

TITLE	ARTIST	ALBUM
Training montage	Harry Gregson-Williams	*Spy Game*
Going on	Gnarls Barkley	*The Odd Couple*
Wrench & Numbers	Jeff Russo	*Fargo* TV series
Let There Be Drums	Incredible Bongo Band	*40yrs of IBB*
Let Them Try	Eric Serra	*The Big Blue*
The Dirty	True Love	*Famous Last Words*
The Lonely Bull	Herb Alpert & Tijuana Brass	*The Lonely Bull*
Paid In Full	Erik B. & Rakim, Marley Marl	*Paid In Full*

Those last two—*The Lonely Bull* and *Paid In Full*—were part of the playlist because they are songs I put into the script. Another thing the gurus love to tell you is you're not allowed to put the names of actual songs into your script.

The reason they give is because song rights are expensive, and if a potential producer reads a scene where you say, "*Pink Floyd's* Wish You Were Here *plays throughout the scene*," a producer will know that song is too expensive and thus, she will pass on your script.

Again, let me destroy their lie by telling you what you're really believing when you subscribe to lies like this . . .

If you are to believe this lie, then that means you believe that a producer could read your script, love every page of it, but pass on it because you had one or two, or five actual songs listed in it. Wow, that would be the dumbest producer on the planet.

No legit producer (or any other entity) is going to pass on your script because you list a real song playing in a scene. It's completely ridiculous and (again) shows how uninformed they are about the real world of Hollywood and how it works.

If you have songs in your script that are far too expensive for the production that is a GOOD PROBLEM to have. Because it means someone is making your movie; someone bought your screenplay. And what will happen is they will have you cut them during the rewrite process.

Placing those songs in your script might have just been the key emotional moment that put the reader across the line to want to buy your script. So, don't ever leave anything out because you "heard" it's a bad idea.

When I create a playlist it can take me less than an hour, or several days. I do it whether I'm writing my own spec script or am on staff writing an episode of television. Yes, even when I'm on a show that has its own soundtrack, I still create my own playlist for the episode I'm writing.

There was an episode I wrote for LEVERAGE, where my fellow writers mocked me because after I was sent to script, meaning cleared to write the episode, I spent days trying to create the right playlist. We usually had about 12–14 days to write our first drafts, and by the time I finally created the playlist I needed, I think I had four days left to write the script. But I did it. When I wrote on NCIS: NEW ORLEANS, my playlists were always very heavily New Orleans music. Blues, jazz, Cajun, zydeco.

The only project I've written where I didn't make a playlist was GEOSTORM. Due to the way in which I was forced to write my version of that script, a playlist wasn't available. Clearly, my writing is better when I have a playlist.

For the heist script, it took me about three hours of going through Spotify, listening to a few seconds of song after song until I had a good hour or more of music. My playlists are living, breathing entities that change throughout my writing. I will drop certain songs and add new ones. But before I can start, I need at least an hour of songs. They can be instrumental or not. I know many writers who can't listen to music with lyrics while they're writing because they say it distracts them. I've never had that problem. I'm too focused on my own words.

Once I have enough songs on the playlist, I can begin the drudgery of phase 5.

PHASE 5: *THE OUTLINE*

People may argue that by outlining, I am "structuring" my story. Again, noun vs. verb. I am probably doing a version of it as far as a court of law might see it, but the important thing is I'm not thinking about it that way. I'm not thinking about stating a theme, incidents, or page count. I'm thinking about my story from the characters' internal POVs as much as possible.

My goal with outlines is to fill the negative space of the beat sheets. For example, I know beat 3 is such-and-such, and I know beat 4 is thus-and-what, so now I need to fill the space between them. Fill it in a way that is organic to the story and the characters. My early outlines are more like advanced beat sheets. My first outline for the heist script contained somewhere around fifteen or so scenes, but nothing with any real detail. Again, I'm building momentum. With each subsequent outline, I get more detailed and fill in more gaps. But my outlines are never too detailed. All I need from them is the map. Some screenwriters write dense, thirty or forty page outlines. I don't want to expend too much creative energy during this phase because I want as much left for the climb up the mountain; the writing of the script.

Eventually, around the third or fourth draft, it starts to look like a real outline. I am not numbering the scenes yet, but I am writing little descriptions of each scene.

How many outlines I do varies from project to project. I've done as many as eight (ugh) when I just couldn't find the rhythm and feel of the piece. I've done as few as three.

For the last outline, I will number the scenes, not for any specific reason other than I like doing it. You do not have to. There are no rules when you're outlining for yourself. When you are under contract to write something for a network or studio, outlining is a required part of the process.

What follows is an example of an "official" outline. It's part of an outline I did for a pilot I wrote for CBS Studios. These need to be much more detailed than the outlines I do for myself.

```
16 - INT. BIG HOUSE - DAY

The following morning, we meet the other Busch women.
Lotsie and Alice are there along with CLARA, young
sister of Dolph and Gussie; MARIE, Gussie's young
wife; and CATHERINE, Dolph's second wife. The entire
room is filled with beautiful, sexy (for 1930s)
dresses. Rose and Alice help Clara try on different
looks as they discuss her chances of being crowned
"Queen of Love & Beauty" at tonight's ball. Clara
lacks confidence, but the others tell her she's a
shoe-in. Only Lotsie speaks the truth by reminding
the group her grandfather was voted "Veiled Profit"
so the odds are pretty good yet another Busch will
wear the crown.
```

```
In the scene we'll glimpse the very distinct
personalities of these women - Marie the blue blood;
Clara sheepish and lacking self-esteem in this
family full of male dominance; Catherine agreeable
and smiling on the surface, but cold and calculating
underneath. When they talk about the company, and the
rival breweries, it's all framed around the women.
They don't discuss the men, they talk of the wives
and daughters of Schlitz and Pabst, and what the end
of prohibition and the looming future means to the
women of this world.
```

You can see this is rather dense. That's because when you write an outline for executives, your goal is to make it very clear what is happening in every scene. They aren't writers, they don't see things as a writer does, so clarity is paramount. That said, most development executives are very smart and creative people. Some not so much. The execs I was blessed to work with on this pilot were some of the smartest I've ever dealt with in my entire career, shoutout to Bryan Seabury and Whitney Berry. But you still need to be clear—they're about to pay you a lot of money, and they need to be sure of what it is they're paying for.

Official outlines are always numbered and sluglined. You may choose not to do that with your own outlines. If nobody is paying you, you can do it any way you see fit.

The outlines I write for my spec work don't look like my official ones. Mine are never as dense because I don't need them to be. What the outline does is serve as my GPS for the story—it isn't for anyone else's eyes. Also, I don't number my scenes until my very last draft. That's because I'm always moving scenes around and it gets annoying to keep renumbering.

Here's a section from one of my outlines for the heist script.

INT. CURTIUS MUSEUM - VAULT ROOM

Estab large vault with infrared beams, etc.

SERVER ROOM - SAME

Oz wedged in small space, watching video on tablet - rat chewing cables.

SECURITY CENTER - SAME

Belgian GUARDS, one young, one old. Young watches feed from CCTV. Old watches bike race on tablet.

Monitors go static.

They speak DUTCH. Young is concerned, but old says it's rats. Young: "Why would rats eat cables?"

SMASH CUT TO:

VENTILATION SYSTEM

Rat straddles a series of cables but it's focused on only one - MOVE IN to show it's covered in a gelatinous substance.

SERVER ROOM

Next to Oz show half-empty Bear-shaped bottle of honey.

Oz lets team know they are good to go.

EXT. CURTIUS MUSEUM - NIGHT

Estab museum, river, and train tracks behind it. FIND Range Rover down street.

INT. RANGE ROVER

Intro Teddy and Hanson, and their watches.

SERVER ROOM

Oz informs them they're on schedule and now they wait, so it's time to play the game. Hanson doesn't want to play.

```
EXT. CURTIUS MUSEUM

Train appears in distance.

Note: make sure to show how quickly crew goes from
joking to complete focus.
```

You can see how much more economical my own outlines are. This is where I think I bridged the gap between writers who think outlining takes away from creative freedom and those who believe they are necessary.

I give myself enough to know what I need to accomplish in the scene, and that's it. You can see I even make notes and ask myself questions. The example above was my second outline. I did another one or two that were about 10%, then 20% more detailed. Then I was ready.

How do I know when it's time to go from outline to script? It's just a feeling and it's unique to every writer. Trust yourself but be self-aware enough to know when you truly feel like it's time rather than you're just sick of outlining and want to start writing. I've made that mistake too many times.

Again, you don't need to outline. If it's not your process, it's not. But in my experience, it makes the writing of the script easier, faster, and more fun.

When you have an outline, when you know where you're going, you can go off on whatever tangents you desire, because all it takes to get back on track is a glance to the outline.

When I have completed my final outline, I put it up on the right side of my computer screen so every time I finish writing a scene, I can cross it off the outline. This is an incredibly motivating psychological hack for screenwriters. Each time you cross off a scene it's a victory and shows you are getting closer and closer to those most beloved two words in a screenwriter's life: FADE OUT.

UNBLENDED and BLENDED OUTLINES

Something I was taught by Barbara Hall and Hart Hanson (on JUDGING AMY) was "blended outlines" and it can be a life-preserver for screenwriters.

When you're writing something that has multiple storylines with multiple characters it can take forever to get a coherent overall outline that encompasses everything you need for your story. Every episode of JUDGING AMY had a minimum of three separate storylines (usually more) and we would create a separate "mini-outline" for each storyline. These were known as unblended outlines. We'd write one for Amy's court case, one for Amy's personal life, one for Amy's mother and her social work case of the week, and whatever else we had going in those fifty pages. Once the showrunners approved each outline on its own, we would blend them together into one outline which became the official outline for the episode sent to the execs.

This is a very productive way to develop your multi-storyline scripts. I've used this technique often, and it's not only a great time-saver, but it ends up helping you begin to see what works and what doesn't for your story. It makes it easier to spot superfluous scenes and characters. When you create unblended outlines for your characters and their storylines, then use those to blend into your overall outline, the process of writing your complete outline goes smoother and ends up being much better.

I did not use the blended outline technique with the heist script because the supporting characters didn't have their own stories so much as they were part of the overall story. But as you'll see, perhaps I should have.

PHASE 6: *WRITING THE SCRIPT*

The best part. The part all writers live for—even the ones who claim to hate writing. This is where the magic happens. My process for the actual writing is very disciplined. I write six days a week. I am up early, usually by 5:30. I have a little meditation and prayer thing I do before anything else, then (if I'm writing at my home office) I make my French Press coffee, and as I wait the four minutes for it to brew, I hit the playlist. The music puts me in the place I need to be, and once I pour that first cup of coffee I begin. I check my outline to see where I left off and get to it.

Sometimes, even when you have an outline, a scene just isn't there yet. Not fully realized in your head. Sometimes you struggle with a scene because things have changed. Perhaps you went off for some rhubarb in Illinois, and now you're four scenes later and realize something isn't working. This is normal, don't panic. Outlines are guides; they don't write the script for you.

When I hit a scene that isn't going well, I move on. I write the scene after that, or if I'm really struggling, I will go to a scene much later in the script—a scene I am particularly excited about or *know*—and write it. Writing something is always better than writing nothing.

Another thing I will do when I struggle is to switch the field. Change the point of attack. When I really need an injection of imagination and freshness, I will go to a hotel. As mentioned, I love writing in hotels. I will spend a day in their lobby or check myself in for a few days or more to write a script. I can't tell you how well this works.

Never be afraid to switch the field.

I work as hard as I can to finish that first draft as quickly as possible. I don't burn through it doing the vomit thing, but I try to keep the momentum rolling. If I get stuck on a page, I will type "xxxx" and move on. I will write scenes out of order, I will use placeholder dialogue, meaning dialogue that's too on the nose, but tells me what will need to be said later with elegantly crafted subtext. I do whatever it takes to keep going. I do the xxxx thing so I can find that section later with a global search. I don't worry about quality at all during the first draft. Nobody but me will ever see it, and its purpose isn't quality.

Here's the thing about first drafts:

Every first draft is perfect because all a first draft needs to be is done.

Let's repeat, bold, and put it in caps . . .

EVERY FIRST DRAFT IS PERFECT BECAUSE ALL A FIRST DRAFT NEEDS TO BE IS DONE.

Even when it feels like it sucks, and trust me, it will suck, just keep going.

I find a lot of newer screenwriters get obsessed with trying to write a first draft that reads like a fifth draft. They go over the same scenes again and again or rewrite the first twenty pages over and over. This is akin to running in place and expecting to get somewhere.

Stop worrying about how good your first draft is. It doesn't need to be good. It doesn't need to be anything but finished. Finish it and it's perfect.

PHASE 7: THE REWRITE

Once I finish a first draft, I put the script away and do not consciously think about it. I work on other stuff, and I've found it's best to work on things that are in no way similar to what I just finished, genre or otherwise. As much as I might want to get back to it, I have learned the longer I'm away, the fresher and more objective I will be when I return. A big mistake I see newer writers make is rewriting too soon. Either they're just so excited to jump back to it, or because they have nothing else to work on, I've seen countless newer scribes go back in too quickly, and thus, they don't see much wrong, don't see much they can cut or improve, so they do a quick pass and think their work is ready for the world.

It isn't.

Avoid going back too soon at all costs.

I will never go back to a first draft in less than a week, and I prefer it to be three to four weeks if life allows.

Rewriting is a very critical phase. You need to be able to objectively look at your earlier draft, kill your darlings, and all that. But you must also be aware of that negative voice in your head, trying to convince you it's all garbage and not worth your time. That same voice you heard around page 62 of your first draft, remember?

Ignore it.

My process for rewriting is in phases, like my overall process. My first phase is to print out a hard copy and find a quality red pen. I will also have one of my trusty Palomino Blackwing pencils standing by if needed.

It's important to understand that at this point I am NOT thinking about writing or rewriting. At this point, I am simply a READER. I read the script as if it were someone else's script sent to me by an agent. This takes focus to do correctly. A lot of times we think we are reading our own work objectively, not realizing that when we come to a scene we absolutely love, our opinion is colored by that love, and thus, we don't read it objectively.

With my hard copy and red pen in hand, I will find a spot where I do not write. I don't read at my desk, at one of my go-to coffee houses, or anywhere else I have written the script. This isn't about writing, it's about reading. When I lived in St. Louis, I had this great apartment 17 floors above the city. My view was insane, and I did some of my best writing (to that point) looking out over the city and Mississippi River. When I would need to pull the red pen out and read, I would sit out on my balcony on the opposite side of my apartment (where I never wrote) with some Highlander Grog coffee from Chauvin Coffee Company, and go to work.

I now live out west on the ground floor. While I no longer have a bird's eye view, I have a lovely koi pond and waterfall, and it's a comfortable, peaceful environment to do this first read. I open the script and READ EVERY WORD. This is another key. Our brains tend to skip ahead when we're reading something we're familiar with. You know what dialogue or description is coming, so you read it, but you don't really read it. Not like someone unfamiliar with the piece. This is why we miss typos. In fact, reading every word out loud is the best way I've found to clear my work of typos.

I read the script as if I were reading a sample to consider hiring someone. And anything I don't like or think could be better, I mark with the red pen. If I find a dialogue exchange or description that's not quite all it can be, I will write four red letters in the margin:

WCDB.

We can do better.

I learned this from the brilliant Karen Hall. It means this is something to come back to during the rewrite because while it might be perfectly fine, I know I can make it better.

That's it, and I keep reading. The red pen isn't for fixing things—it's for identifying things that need to be fixed *later*. I read the whole script like this. The most specific I'll get during this part of the process is if a line of dialogue or description just comes to me in the moment of reading, I will make a note of it. But that's rare. Any typos I find I circle. The only other thing I do with the red pen is to cross out. The first of many darlings to be slain. Crossing out a line, a transition, a tag, or an entire scene I know is not needed.

I always try to finish this first read in one sitting. It just makes things tougher if you stop and start this process.

Once I have read the entire thing and marked up the script, I put it away, but not for long. I want to keep all the thoughts and ideas I have from the read as fresh as possible. That said, I have learned the hard way it's best not to go immediately into the rewrite. I've just expelled a lot of precious creative energy reading and marking up an entire screenplay, so I like to give myself some time to recharge.

I usually try to do that first red pen read in the morning. That way I can take a break, maybe have some lunch or something and then settle in at the keyboard in the afternoon.

I put the marked-up hard copy next to my keyboard and I go from page one.

This is the first actual rewrite. When you try to rewrite something without having read through the entire thing, it's a slog, and you often create more work than necessary for yourself.

My first rewrite is nothing more than addressing all my red pen marks. Fixing typos, working on the WCDB parts, and generally just making it a little better, a little tighter. I am NOT trying to write a ready-for-Hollywood script with my second draft. That's self-inflicted pain. I have made peace with the fact this process takes time, and everything will be better for it. Patience is the screenwriter's friend.

Once I've gone through the whole script, I (again) put the thing away. This time just for a couple of days max. But during this time, I am not thinking about it at all.

The next phase is the second rewrite or what is (in reality) the Third Draft. This one involves some heavy lifting.

I again print out a new hard copy, grab my red pen, and read. I can do this in my office, or wherever, it doesn't matter because now I am writing while I read.

This is a rewrite.

I will go through the script focused solely on story. Does the story work? Does it hold up? Does it track? Does it make sense? I'm not worried about any character stuff that isn't directly pushing the story forward.

I call this rewrite the Story Rewrite.

Pretty creative, eh?

Once I've completed this rewrite, I will decide if I feel it's ready for other people's eyes. There are four people I send my first drafts to. Only it's not my first or even second draft. It's actually my third draft, but for them it's a first draft. My four people are all working professional screenwriters. They are all friends to varying degrees, and we all share our stuff with each other.

If I decide to send this out, two of the four people get it. I save two of them for the next draft. This is partially because I don't want too many notes/thoughts/ideas at this point, and because these last two are very successful, very busy screenwriters, and I know I can only ask them to read one time.

Something I heard Brain Koppelman once say, and absolutely agree with is:

> *"An amateur screenwriter only wants to hear what's good about their script; a professional only wants to hear what's bad."*

What this means is we (professionals) don't need to be coddled or validated. We have confidence in our writing through our experience. We are not interested in hearing how amazing our script is (though, that's lovely a thing) as much as we want to hear what's *not* working. What we can make better. One common denominator in most all the working professionals I know is we all want to be better. Whether we're at Steve Zaillian's level or we're a story editor in our second year in the biz, we all want to get better.

What we want, what we need from a fellow writer's notes is what might not be working, or how something might work better. No matter how much time we give ourselves away from our work, we can never be as objective as someone who didn't write it. The reason I give my work only to fellow professionals is because I can trust them. Not just how to identify good and bad writing, but they understand the process. They know what an early draft is versus a production draft, etc. I have shared my work with non-writing professionals as well as people not connected to the business in any way, but never early drafts like this, and I am never looking for anything from them. I usually only give things out to folks if they request it for a social read.

It's completely fine to give your dark, dystopian screenplay to your Aunt Betty, but I would caution you against taking her notes about it being too dark and too dystopian. Same for giving your lighthearted, all-about-the-love romantic comedy to your co-worker who's been divorced three times, has a TRO against them, and just got dumped. The notes they give you about your story being complete bullshit might be a bit . . . tainted.

Once I get notes back from my two readers, I will go through them and decide which I want to address and which I don't. I will often take most of the notes because I trust these folks. I know them as people and as screenwriters, and they know me.

My next rewrite will implement these notes, and then I'll do another READ. I get my French Press coffee, go to my non-writing space, and read the script doing my best to (again) be a first-time objective reader. I mark stuff with the red pen, and then that same day it's onto the next rewrite.

Once that one is complete (I told you, this gig is a marathon, not a sprint) the rewrite that follows is technically draft five.

This rewrite is solely character.

All I focus on is character. Character behavior, dialogue, relationships, reactions, you name it. I don't worry about descriptions, locations, settings, or overall story machinations. I'm just looking at each character and making sure they are as unique and authentic as possible, and that their own personal journey tracks through my story.

This is the draft where I try to make sure someone can read the script and know which character is speaking without having their name above the dialogue.

Finally, we come to draft six. The draft six rewrite is THE WRITING draft. I'm going through all my descriptions, all my language and syntax, all my turns of phrase, all the writing. Once this draft is finished, I give it to the other two fellow professionals. When I get their notes, I do one more pass and then (usually) my script is ready to be read by agents, managers, lawyers, producers, executives, whomever.

Yes, your math is correct. I never send anything out that hasn't been rewritten at least six times. Sometimes more.

When I sent the heist script out to my final two readers, I was very excited. I could not wait to hear their thoughts, do whatever quick polish was needed, and get it to my reps. One of my readers was unavailable, so it only went to the other, John Rogers. A veteran feature writer, showrunner, and one of the best screenwriters I know. I trust his judgment completely.

And he didn't like it.

Well, that's not really accurate. He loved it, but there was just one problem . . .

My main character. My protagonist.

John didn't care about him. He didn't feel like the character was anywhere near as well-defined and three-dimensional as all the others. Thus, his relationships with the other characters weren't there. John felt the script needed a complete rewrite with a whole new version of my protagonist.

I was devastated.

It's good to hear something like this about an early draft, but this was the fifth or sixth draft. It was a massive blow to my writer ego. I was imagining Idris Elba and Emily Blunt being directed by JJ Abrams with Megan Ellison producing, and all of us sitting on set in Singapore having the greatest time . . . exactly what one should not be thinking about until it actually happens. I had committed the cardinal sin of screenwriting: I had fallen in love with what the outcome *could* be, rather than focusing on writing the best story.

I knew the only thing I could do was walk away. I was too close to it. I had lost my perspective. I put the script away and moved on with my life. I took another paid gig and began writing another spec. Six months later I pulled out the script, read it and read John's notes.

He was 100% correct. My protagonist was an empty shell of a derivative character surrounded by a bunch of wonderful characters having three-dimensional relationships with each other. My protag was a fencepost.

Ugh.

By this time, I had walked it off. That's the term I use when a writer gets rejected. Either their spec hits the market and doesn't sell, their movie opens and flops, their series gets canceled, their pilot isn't picked up, or any of the million other ways a screenwriter's world can implode. You take the hit, and you walk it off. Sometimes it's an internal walk, sometimes it's literal. When I went to see GEOSTORM on opening night at the Sherman Oaks Galleria, I hadn't seen a cut in two years. I had no idea what to expect. I sat in that dark theater as the credits rolled completely atrophied. Only after the lights came on did I leave . . . and I walked it off. I walked up and down Ventura Boulevard that Friday night for over an hour.

ASIDE: Friends of mine have heard me mock GEOSTORM (*#Guyotstorm*), and while there are certainly debatable issues with the finished product, I learned from Scott Rosenberg to never take sides against the family. It's like Omerta. Regardless of how bad a finished film or series may be in your eyes; you never publicly trash a project with your name on it. It is insanely difficult to get a motion picture made, let alone released, and whether it ends up being amazing or awful, one should always take pride in accomplishing such a rarefied feat.

But I am honest about my work. I'm self-aware. I know when I've written something well, when I haven't, and when something I did write well ended up awful by the time it made it to the screen. What you will never hear me say is that something (anything) I've written is better than something someone else has written, even if I believe it to be true. While all art is subjective, to publicly state for example that some script I've written is "nearly perfect" and better than, say, MEMENTO, would be ridiculous at best, and arrogantly delusional at worst . . . meow.

Back to my process with the heist script. Six months after getting those notes from John I went back in. I did a total page one rewrite. And something magical happened. It worked.

This story had been with me for so long, and I had so much passion for it, I had written all those previous drafts for the tiny little movie theater inside my head. Now, let me be clear—you should always write the story you want to tell; the movie you want to see. But take care not to get lost in your passion. The reason I missed such an obvious flaw in my writing was that I had been writing this thing as a watch fanboy, not as a professional screenwriter. I was all about the watches, not about the people.

When I went back in, I did so as a working professional screenwriter.

I focused on why John didn't care about my character of Dane.

And despite being a working professional for decades at this point, I realized I had written this "really cool" character, but I had forgotten it's not about the characters we create . . . it's about their relationships with the other characters that make a story compelling. As I began to dive into Dane's relationship with the others in the story, it got better, and eventually, I realized I was writing about fathers and sons. While the story had a father and son in it, I was too focused on the bright shiny objects of the story to see what was INSIDE the story. Once I focused on that, everything changed. I rewrote scenes focused on the relationships and not just the surface stuff. Instead of a scene where Dane says cool things to another character, I wrote a scene where two humans are talking to each other, and the way they do it is based on who they are and the history of their relationship. Things that may not be in the script. Some call this backstory; I refer to it as "Act Zero stuff." All the stuff that happened in the world BEFORE the first page of the screenplay.

This new rewrite flowed, and that does not happen very often. In my experience, I'd say for every project that takes, say, six months of your life to write—from outline to `FADE OUT`—you can expect maybe four or five days of truly great writing. Where you're in that flow state and everything is fluid. Four days out of six months is a victory.

When I went back in on the heist script, I finished the rewrite in about three weeks, having a good seven or eight days in the flow state.

I humbly asked John if he would read the new draft. He was glad to do it. Waiting for his notes was excruciating. I tried to work on other stuff, but I continuously checked my inbox for his email. Eventually, it came.

He blessed the script. I had done it. And in doing so, I made other parts of the story better. Once I had a solid three-dimensional protagonist whom the reader empathized with, everything else leveled up. The new version of this character talked differently, behaved differently, reacted, and responded differently, and thus, all the relationships in the story did so as well. All for the betterment of the script.

The heist script has since generated enough interest from actors and producers that, at the time of this writing, negotiations are happening. Hopefully, it will see the light of a 20K. But that sentence right there may have put the hex on it. After all, this is Hollywood where nothing is guaranteed except that there are never, ever any guarantees.

When it comes to my process for writing something under contract (as opposed to on spec) it is no different. As an example from my time as the Co-Executive Producer on NCIS: NEW ORLEANS, I give you Season 4, Episode 16, "Empathy":

First, *Empathy* is a terrible title. It's so incredibly on the nose, so clinical, so lacking in mystery, intrigue, you name it, and to top it off, not really what the episode was about.

I wanted to call the episode "Requiem," but there was another episode that title was better suited for, so then I came up with "Gray Matter." It went through all the stages of concept, outline, etc., with that title. After I turned in the first draft of the script the showrunner inexplicably changed the title to "Empathy." When I asked why, his response was something along the lines of, "Because it's about empathy."

Uh, no. But his show, not mine.

That's part of writing on someone else's show. The showrunner I worked with on this series wasn't the most creative cat, but even when they don't seem to *get it,* even when they make bad choices creatively or otherwise, even when you know what they want is not good for the show, you must roll with it. Or they will quickly get someone who will roll, like a dung beetle going downhill.

HOW IT STARTED

This was during the second half of season four, and I had already made the decision I was going to leave the show. It was a toxic work environment, creativity wasn't encouraged, and while it paid well and gave you street cred within the TV world, I was miserable. Because of all this, I decided the last episode I wrote of this giant franchise procedural was going to matter. At least to me.

I had lost my father to Alzheimer's earlier, and I wanted to say something about it. This had nothing to do with NCIS: NEW ORLEANS. I wanted to say something for myself. For my late father. As writers we need to have something to say, otherwise, what's the point? Why do it at all? Clearly, my relationship with my father informs my writing. And now, I wanted to honor him.

The showrunner at the time loved to ask, "*What's the poster?*" Meaning, if the episode had a One Sheet—a movie poster—what would it be? It was his way of breaking story. He needed to find a movie from history that we could use as shorthand for the episode idea we were pitching.

An example of this would be if a writer pitched the idea of Pride (the character played by Scott Bakula) having to race to find and dismantle a bomb before it blows up the entire city, the writer pitching said idea would have to give the showrunner a movie title or titles that were along the same plot lines so the showrunner could see the idea in his mind.

In my humble opinion, this isn't the best way to come up with story. It makes everything you do derivative, which I guess is fine if you're doing a giant broadcast franchise where every episode needs to be basically the same. But if you want to make great television, and tell great stories, it's lacking.

But it wasn't my show.

One of my strengths is I have a good understanding of human behavior, and I can read people fairly well. At this point in the season, I had a pretty good read on the showrunner, what he liked and didn't like, and what his idea of coloring outside the lines was. For him, coloring outside the lines was nothing more than a poster for a movie that was either critically acclaimed but not well known, or a foreign film. I remembered seeing a brilliant Belgian thriller called DE ZAAK ALZHEIMER (AKA THE MEMORY OF A KILLER) about an aging hitman who was struggling with Alzheimer's. I used that poster to pitch my idea to the showrunner. A hitman is in New Orleans to off a congressional aid but seems to be killing the wrong targets. The showrunner was intrigued but couldn't see how it could be an episode of the show. Enter my fellow writers on staff. As the room began to discuss the idea, we came up with how the NCIS team would all want to take this nasty hitman down, but Pride being omniscient isn't so quick to jump on board. Pride is so much smarter than any other character on television that he can sense something isn't right with the hitman.

Eventually, we learn the folks the hitman is killing are other hitmen sent to take out a congressional aid, and the team must learn why. My idea was the hitman is a war hero who went bad, and as Alzheimer's begins to spread through his brain, he forgets the hitman part of himself and remembers the war hero part. That's an oversimplification, but you get the idea.

I pitched how we could connect this emotionally to our lead character. What if Pride's mother suffers from Alzheimer's? This was initially met with pushback because, despite the fact we were in the fourth season of the series, Pride's mother had never been spoken about other than a couple of vague references about his past. This happens often in series writing; a character's backstory will be established in dialogue early on without thinking about how that might make things difficult for the writing staff down the road. However, the room (meaning the writing staff) managed to come up with something that could work as to why Pride's mom was never in the show, or even talked about . . . she was off in another country getting very specialized medical care, and Pride being Pride has kept it to himself.

Great! My plan of creative subterfuge was unfolding!

We had to turn in what is called a "two-pager" before the showrunners and execs could approve a story to go forward. It was basically a short treatment/synopsis of the episode (not more than two pages long), and something that is not uncommon in the TV world. On my first episode for NCIS: NOLA, I really struggled with the two-pager to the point I even considered walking away from the gig. Even though we were only six or so episodes into the season, I was already aware how dysfunctional it was on several levels. One of the many reasons I was unhappy was because while there was one showrunner, there were two Executive

Producers who both acted in a showrunner capacity depending on what day it was. When this is done right, it can be very productive in splitting up the massive amount of showrunning duties between two people. On this show, however, the two people were almost polar opposites when it came to not just showrunning but writing and storytelling. They broke story differently, and they preferred you write things their way . . . so we literally had to alter the way we wrote depending on which EP was overseeing our episode. What would be approved by one of them would often be rejected by the other. This was extremely counterproductive, not to mention frustrating from a creative POV. The biggest problem in a situation like this, and what caused most issues on this show was something that is possibly the single most common problem on all Hollywood productions . . .

Lack of communication.

Let me rephrase—lack of communication *on purpose.*

Hollywood is filled with insecurity—that's why most of us become creatives—and one of the ways insecurity manifests itself is by people never wanting to be held accountable for their actions, opinions, and decision-making.

You know how the explosion of social media has led to a global population of folks hiding behind the anonymity of a keyboard as they spout all their opinions, rage, and didactic rhetoric? That's been happening in Hollywood for decades. Only instead of hiding behind some social media avatar they hide behind other people. When there is a metaphorical fire to be put out or a problem to be handled on a production, nobody wants to have face-to-face meetings or conference calls about it. Instead, they form these little mini-meetings and blame the people who are over in the other mini-meetings for whatever went wrong and take credit for whatever went right. Nobody wants to risk being held accountable for what they said, did, or didn't do . . . unless something good happened. Then they're the first to take credit.

I remember when I was in charge during the second season of THE LIBRARIANS. We were shooting up in Portland, Oregon, and most members of the producing team refused to ever be on a call together, let alone in the same room. Someone would claim there was a problem with so-and-so's department, or so-and-so says this or is doing such-and-such. Any time I tried to get everyone in the same room to solve the problems, no one wanted any part of it. None of them wanted to be held accountable for their actions, words, gossip, lies, you name it.

When it came to the dueling EPs on NCIS: NOLA, both would talk to the writing staff about the faults of the other one, but neither had the sack to confront the other one or be accountable for their own actions or opinions. The staff was constantly thrown under the bus by both EPs in order to keep either one from ever having to take responsibility for what they said, did, or didn't do. That's how it went with everything from the two-pagers to the outlines to the writing of the scripts. Depending on which EP was assigned to oversee your episode, it could go smoothly, or be like using sandpaper on an open wound.

My first two-pager was sandpaper.

It was rejected again and again for not being "right," without any direction as to what *right* actually was, or why it wasn't right. It was just wrong.

Finally, the EP covering that episode became so frustrated with me that he wrote the two-pager himself—exactly the *right* way. When I read his version, it was literally the same as my last two attempts. Literally, all that was done was rearrange the language of my sentences, so they became *his* sentences.

But not my show.

I want to note for the record that despite how you may be interpreting my tone here, I say all this without any animosity or contempt. Because this is the gig. It's what we sign up for when we become television writers. It's the life. When you are working on someone else's show, you do it their way or they will find someone who will. This is a big reason why yes-men do so well in Hollywood, especially in television. People prefer yes-men over talent.

When it came time to write my two-pager for the episode about my father, I was obviously nervous because of my previous experience. Also, it was later in the season and at this point morale in the writers room was low. Like, Death Valley low. However, it was the other EP covering this episode and my two-pager was approved (using my own sentences), and I was off to outline.

THE OUTLINE

Please note I skipped over the actual breaking of the episode that happened in the writers room. I pitched the concept, the showrunner approved it, and then the room set to breaking the story—which means all of us came up with the scenes for the episode and how they would unfold. Scene by scene, from the opening crime—part of the formula of the show—to the NCIS team being called in, to whatever other storylines we needed to integrate into the episode, all the way through to the end.

Let me say here that breaking an episode in a room full of talented writers can be one of the most invigorating activities, especially when you have a quality showrunner driving things. When you're in a room of not-so-talented writers, and/or a room where the showrunner rarely makes an appearance before noon, it can be one of the most frustratingly difficult things to accomplish. The staff on NOLA was great. We had several very talented writers in the room. Despite having a pair of EPs who rarely showed up when the rest of us did, the staff rallied together and did the best we could every episode. I would work with any of those writers again.

The only real change in my story I had to accept was the powers that be didn't want the hitman to be a victim of Alzheimer's. I forget why, but it was something about risking the network or the audience being offended . . . or something. So, we went with brain tumor.

The hitman had a brain tumor which gave him all the symptoms of Alzheimer's, but he didn't have Alzheimer's!

Whatever. Not my show.

Once the story was broken, and the two-pager done, it was time for me to do some actual screenwriting. And the first thing one must do on all television shows is write the outline. An outline is required for several reasons. First, it's for the studio and network execs to have an idea of how the episode will "look." They get to read each scene and give their thoughts (pro and con) on individual acts, scenes, storylines, character moments, you name it. Sometimes their notes are superfluous and silly, but more often than you would think from all the stories you hear, their notes are good.

When you complete an outline for an episode of television you don't have much freedom to go off course in the writing because the outline has been given not only to the studio and network but to department heads in the production. Everyone from the DP to the costume designer to the prop department and so on is already working based on what's in your outline. Making one-hour dramatic television is basically making a feature film every two weeks without stopping. Once the train leaves the station—the train being your outline—there is no backing it up.

In series television, the outline is literally a scene-by-scene description. Every scene that will be in the episode is first agreed to in the writers room and put up on a card or whiteboard, or however that room works. For broadcast shows, the scenes are usually broken up by the "acts" which (as discussed) are not acts at all, but rather inorganic breaks in the episode where the network drops in their advertisers' commercials.

These have come to be known as "Act Breaks" in the industry which has led to the INCORRECT assumption that they are actual act breaks in the story's structure. They are not. They exist only in the world of marketing and advertising, not in story.

The good news about the outline phase is this is where the writer's individual process kicks in. As I said, when you write on someone else's show, it can be a wonderful, inspiring experience, or it can be an awful, even traumatic experience. Either way, you must adapt, or you will be out. You must adapt to what and how they want you to write—but however that is, your process is still your own process, and your Voice is still your Voice.

Before I began the outline, I had to create my playlist. Once I had the playlist going, I pulled the cards from the writers room. Some writers take photos of the cards on the board, some writers make multiple trips into the room to stare at the cards, whatever works, works. When I'm on script, I prefer writing somewhere other than the office, so I will have a photo of the cards with me. The cards for each scene are just a shorthand of what's in that scene. Here's what the very first card looked like for this episode:

```
EXT. RIVERWALK - NIGHT

Fake agents stop woman. About to abduct her when
mystery man takes them out.
```

That's it. That's all that was on the card. Now, here's that same scene as it looked in the official outline:

```
COLD OPEN

EXT. RIVERWALK - NIGHT

Empty. Spooky. Find a woman, MOLLY LINDELL, walking
with purpose. Someone whistles, and she turns - sees
two MEN IN SUITS. They call her by name, beckon
her over. Molly hesitates until she sees their
credentials... NCIS AGENTS.

She lets out a breath and goes to them. As she
approaches, ANOTHER MAN appears out of nowhere and
attacks the two agents. One agent pulls his gun, but
the mystery man, in one lightning move, snatches the
gun, breaking the man's elbow, then BAM! BAM! Puts
two rounds into the agent. The second agent can't
even get his weapon out before the mystery man is on
him like a python, and we hear that dreaded SNAP of
the man's neck, and he falls dead. Molly, frozen in
terror, tries to scream, but the mystery man covers
her mouth, and in a flash they're out of frame... off
the two dead bodies on the ground - SMASH TO CREDITS
```

Before any of you ask about the "cold open," let me explain. For an episode of television like this, the outline must be very specific. Looking back at mine for this episode, it was 12 pages, consisting of a COLD OPEN, TEASER, and then four ACTS. Those were all NCIS: NOLA-specific terms and requirements. If you're writing your own spec pilot, don't put those in. They aren't needed, and will just annoy the reader.

I write out each scene the same way I wrote the first one, basically describing everything that is happening within the scene. Sometimes I'll add dialogue. It doesn't matter if that dialogue ends up in the script. Sometimes it does, sometimes it doesn't.

I want to show you the final scene of this episode's outline, but before I do, I think it's important to give you a little backstory . . .

When my father was in the throes of this vicious disease, it was really rough. For any of you who've experienced a loved one suffering from Alzheimer's, you know what I'm talking about. It's brutally heartbreaking just trying to have a conversation. Yet, in my father's case, and I don't know if this is common among patients, there would be these moments, these tiny little triggers where the person seems to come out of their fog briefly. At least that's what happened with my father. And what would bring him out was the theme music of MONDAY NIGHT FOOTBALL.

My father and I loved MONDAY NIGHT FOOTBALL, and I can't count how many games we watched together. Once I grew up and left the house, I made a point of always—no matter where I was or what I was going through—being home with him to watch the first Monday night game of each season.

As my father fell deeper into the darkness of the disease, things got rough for our family and me. But in what I can only credit God with, whenever I would show up for that MONDAY NIGHT FOOTBALL game and those first four notes of *Heavy Action* (the iconic theme music of Monday Night Football composed by Johnny Pearson) would kick in, my father would return. His eyes would light, and for just a bit he was back. He would look at me with recognition, he would understand. It never lasted long, but that music would play, the crowd would roar, the announcers would blather, and we would go back in time . . . a father and son watching football together.

I wanted to tell that story. And I was committed to doing it inside the chains of a broadcast procedural.

I pitched the idea that Pride calls his mom every week. Something that we've never seen on the show before but happens. Off screen. And his mother doesn't recognize Pride's voice, doesn't recognize it's her son. But then he plays a song for her, and something happens. Thankfully, Scott Bakula is a musician and loved music being part of Pride's life and character. So, Pride plays a song over the phone and his mother recognizes it. And she begins to play as well. They play this beautiful little tune together from his childhood. And for that moment, Dwayne Pride and his mother playing music are . . . Paul Guyot and his father watching MONDAY NIGHT FOOTBALL.

My episode was approved. I wrote it the same way I wrote the heist script, only with fewer rewrites before turning it in. And thanks be to God, the script wasn't rewritten by the showrunner much at all. Yes, the title was changed, but as I've said, not my monkey, not my circus.

Once I finished the outline and the EPs were happy with it, it went to the studio and network. On most shows the studio gets the outlines and scripts before the network. They give you their notes, always qualifying them with some version of, "*This is what the network wants.*" They are always wrong. The studio and network rarely want the same thing.

On this show the studio and network were basically the same entity. Different people in different offices, but all under the same corporate umbrella. Not great for creativity, but efficient when it comes to cutting down on meaningless notes.

Once the outline is officially blessed, it's off to script.

As far as deviating from the outline, as I said, when it comes to working on a television series the outline is somewhat sacred. You can deviate insomuch as potential dialogue or possible blocking, but as far as locations, most actions, and which characters are or aren't in the scene, you're stuck. I use this boxing in as a challenge. In exposition scenes (which all procedurals have) I always did my best to hide the exposition in character reveal. Meaning, I would find ways to get out the needed exposition without it seeming like exposition, or at least without it seeming like the proverbial Man with a Hat stepping onto the stage.

Sometimes I would pull off something I was proud of. Other times I'd go too far, and the EPs or execs would give a note that the scene needed to be "clearer" which is exec-speak for dumbing it down. Clarity is an important part of screenwriting and storytelling, but the word clarity is often tossed around by television executives because they don't want to be on record as saying something like, "*You need to dumb it down because we underestimate the intelligence of our audience and don't want to offend anyone by making them feel intellectually inferior.*"

NCIS: NEW ORLEANS prided itself (pun slightly intended) on being the "character-driven" show of the franchise. While all the NCIS shows were part of the NCIS family (read: franchise) the Nola clan firmly believed it to be the best as far as character. I can't speak to this because I have never seen an episode of NCIS: LOS ANGELES or NCIS: HAWAII and have only seen one episode of the mothership, NCIS.

While I can't give you actual excerpts here of the scripts (due to some bizarre legal reasons) I can give you a quick example of what I'm talking about.

Let's say you need your characters to tell the audience the person they are looking for is a white male in his fifties who has a history of drug-related offenses as well as assault and battery. The tried-and-true broadcast network way to do this is to simply have one character say all that. Perhaps they're reading it off a rap sheet or something. Then another character will say something like, "*Sounds like a real charmer.*"

How I might write that scene is as follows:

```
INT. OFFICE - DAY

Dale and Lola join Calvin in the office.

                    CALVIN
              (hits the remote)
          John Smith.

On the flatscreen appears a mugshot of a white male
with scraggly white hair and beard. Meet JOHN SMITH.

                    LOLA
          Looks like Santa Claus on meth.

                    CALVIN
          Close. Five pops for dealing.

                    DALE
          Santa needs to attend some anger
          management courses, too.
              (re: the screen)
          Three assault and battery charges.

                    LOLA
          Well, kids at the mall can be annoying.
```

Obviously, how you write it depends on the tone of the show and other factors. On most one-hour shows the writer has anywhere from ten days to two weeks or so to complete their first draft. As the season rolls on, that writing window gets smaller because once production on episode one begins, you're shooting episodes every week, and it's all you can do to remain on schedule.

You turn your first draft into the EPs. If it's early and there's time, they give you notes and you take another pass. Maybe even a second pass if time allows. If it's later in the season, it's likely you may not get to do any more work after your first draft, depending on your level on staff. Lower-level writers such as story editors won't get as many rewrite opportunities as upper levels like Supervising Producers and Co-Executive Producers. Not because of any elitist malfeasance, but simply for time and efficiency. An upper-level writer has much more experience with writing under the strains of short deadlines and can get things done quicker.

I want to say a couple of things here. As mentioned, my time on the show wasn't the best, but this episode was a fantastic experience. Looking back, I believe a lot of what made it so good was because I was mentally and emotionally in the *No Fucks Given* mode I had learned years before on my first series. When you can have that mindset during any storms that besiege you, it certainly helps. I wasn't in fear of losing my job; I wasn't worried about offending anyone or getting on the bad side of anyone in a leadership role; I was simply focused on *being a writer.* Telling the story I needed to tell.

The episode was good. Whether you have any respect for giant broadcast procedurals, I'm very proud of it. What I am the proudest of, and what is my single greatest memory of that turbulent frustrating year on the show, is when we shot that final scene down in New Orleans. Here's the scene from the outline, and this is one of those rare occasions where the way I wrote it in the outline is almost exactly how it was in the script, and ended up on-screen:

```
INT. PRIDE'S BAR - DAY

Pride sits at the piano... dials his phone... after a
moment someone answers... "Hey, mama. It's Dwayne..."
then says, "Dwayne, your son..." We hear her frail
voice say, "Who?" A flash of pain in Pride's eyes...
it hurts so much.

He begins to play... an old French ballad. Pride
plays, sings softly... he pauses, waiting, hoping
to hear something from the phone... nothing. He
continues on... and then... he hears it. She is
playing her piano... like old times. Mother and son
playing together... for this moment, she remembers.

Pride smiles as they play...

                                        FADE OUT
```

Tessa Blake directed the episode, and she was an absolute gem to work with. She understood what I was trying to sneak into the show, and she was on board. And God bless Scott Bakula. He got it, too. He even protected the episode (and me) once or twice when the powers that be became nervous and wanted to dumb down or flatten out the storyline.

My best moment was when we were in New Orleans on the last day of the shoot. Things had gone well, the regular and guest cast were great, the crew was fantastic as always, the weather had been decent, all was good.

We were on our soundstages, inside Pride's apartment. Bakula had composed the song he was going to play in that final scene. It was a sweet, melancholy number with a French edge to it. Perfect for the character and the scene. Pride calls his mother overseas and when she gets on the phone, she doesn't know who he is. We see in Pride's face that this is the norm, and it destroys him. But he remains strong and patient and continues on. He begins to play the song—the song they shared during his childhood—and after a moment we hear a piano on the other end . . . his mother. Playing along with her son.

I remember I had moved away from video village to watch. I didn't know how it was going to affect me emotionally, and I didn't want to seem like anything but a professional. I found a place behind a 4x Floppy where I could look to my right and see Tessa at the monitors and look to my left to see Bakula doing the scene. I was on an apple box in my nice little cocoon . . . when a large member of the grip department came and sat right next to me.

Swell.

This guy had been listening earlier in the week when Bakula and I were discussing my father and the impetus of this episode. I'm sure he was trying to be supportive of me, but all I wanted in that moment was to be alone.

Tessa called action and the scene began. Bakula was masterful. The scene itself was beautiful, and for me, transcendent. I did my best to hold it together as I watched, remembering those Monday nights with my late father.

Tessa called "*Cut*," and the entire stage was silent. Bakula looked for me. His eyes found mine and without a word, he asked me if it was good. I smiled and nodded. He winked at me and nodded back.

And I began to cry.

The grip put his arm around me and was saying something about when he lived in Hawaii with some dog and . . . then Tessa came over and hugged me. I hugged her back. For a long time.

It was the culmination of my career to that point, which may sound exaggerated or dramatic, but within the very personal context of what this was all about, and the fact I'd managed to pull it off in this giant machine, it was.

That's my writing process, folks. Yours is likely different. No two are the same, and there is not one right way to do it. The only right way is whatever works best for you. So, try different things. Try writing in different places at different times until you find what works best. The one thing I recommend you do the same as myself (and most all working professional screenwriters) is be disciplined.

This concludes most of the practical How-To stuff in this book. I'm sure some of you are feeling cheated or let down. *Where's the stuff I can print out and follow? Where are the charts or circles or steps to follow to be great?*

Sorry.

They aren't here because those are lies, and this book is about truth.

I do have some cool writing exercises coming up, and I can attest they have worked for me as well as other professionals.

If you're feeling good (or not so good) at this point, but still wondering how to get started with this screenwriting dream of yours, or how to improve your current screenwriting journey, I will say the first thing to do is unlearn all the sewage that's been force fed into your system all these years.

Other than that . . .

Keep writing.

12

WRITING EXERCISES

I KNOW WRITERS who think "exercises" are pointless. They say just put your butt in the chair and work. While I understand their point of view, I believe writing exercises can help build writing muscles just as physical exercises build literal muscles. What's true in both endeavors is one must commit. You will never get healthy by half-assing workouts, and you will never become the healthiest (best) screenwriter you can be without consistently working your writing muscles.

You don't lift once or twice a month and then expect to look like Aldis Hodge. Just like you shouldn't tackle a writing exercise once or twice, then expect to be penning Sorkinian tales. To that end, you shouldn't write one or two screenplays and expect his level of ability. It could happen, you might be blessed beyond measure with supreme storytelling talent, but the odds are against it. So, why not hit the writing gym and increase your odds?

What follows are exercises working professionals screenwriters have engaged in which have produced quality results.

WRITER CROSSTRAINING

This first one is easy. If you're struggling with your screenplay, and you've tried all the tricks and dodges to find momentum, try writing in a form *other* than screenwriting.

Work on a short story. Write a blog post—even if you don't have a blog. Work on a play. Write an essay, or journal entry. Write an email to someone you haven't spoken to in years—you don't have to send it.

If all else fails, write about not being able to write. Personally, I find short stories to be great instigators of screenwriting creativity. They are probably the closest thing the prose world has to what we do, but writing prose is so freaking freeing compared to screenwriting. No sluglines, no parentheticals, no centering dialogue, no transitions. Just writing. Your mileage may vary, but just try something, anything. Writing ANYTHING is better than sitting at your keyboard and writing nothing.

As Jodie Picoult said, "*You can edit a bad page, you can't edit a blank page.*"

Writing begets writing.

DOING THE DOZENS

Not *those* Dozens. This is something I turned a couple of my professional screenwriter mates onto, and they report quality results. What's cool about it is that you can use it during the outline phase, the treatment phase, the screenplay phase, the rewrite phase, any time you're a bit bogged down with a scene or story that doesn't feel fresh, something not seen or written a thousand times before. Here's how it works:

Take a situation, any situation. It can be how two characters meet, or a chase scene, or a breakup. Any scenario you want. Write twelve different ways it could happen. Let's go with how two characters could meet.

1. At baggage claim inside an airport
2. On line at a coffee place
3. A car accident

And so on.

Here's a chase scene:

1. Running on top of a building
2. On bicycles through city streets at rush hour
3. Down a ski slope *without* skis

You get the picture.

The thing is, you have to write twelve. Not ten, not twenty. Twelve. Don't ask me why, but twelve is the sweet spot.

And here's the most important part—it doesn't matter if the ideas are good, bad, cliché, sappy, lame, genius, whatever. That's not the point. The point is you are generating creativity in your writer brain to then harness and infuse into your screenplay.

Write your twelve different versions, and what usually happens is one of them is so great you put it into your script, and off you go! Back on the writing train! Or . . . all twelve suck, but you're inspired to do better, and thus, you're off and running trying to do better. Or . . . none of them are quite right, but number five spurs something in your mind about another scene you have early in your script, and you go to it with new inspiration and motivation.

Trust me, doing the dozens works.

AT THE BAR

This one has been around a while and can be called a couple of different things, but At The Bar is the most common, and the name I use.

The idea is when you're struggling with a scene, be it the emotional resonance, the actual dialogue, the point where it belongs in your story, the physical location or setting of the scene, or whatever it is you're finding difficult to navigate, you take two of your characters and sit them at a bar.

You literally write the slugline `INT. BAR – NIGHT` and put two of your characters next to each other. Then you have them talk about whatever it is you're struggling with.

Say you need a scene where your protagonist confronts your antagonist for the first time, and you haven't figured out when or how they come together. Or maybe you've written the scene once or multiple times, but what you have just isn't working for you. Try At The Bar.

```
INT. BAR - NIGHT

Carl and Jasper sit at the bar.

                    CARL
          I don't know how we're supposed to meet.

                    JASPER
          What about after I kill Bob?

                    CARL
          You're gonna kill Bob?

                    JASPER
          Was thinking about it, yeah.

Carl sips his bourbon, considering.

                    CARL
          I'm the hero, I shouldn't let you do that.

                    JASPER
          Maybe that's how we meet?

                    CARL
          When you kill Bob?

                    JASPER
          Yeah. I'm hacking him up, and-

                    CARL
          -I come in and kick your ass and save him!

                    JASPER
          Well, not sure about the ass kic-

                    CARL
          -That's a great idea, Jasp!
               (to the bartender)
          Get him another one on me!
```

This is obviously an overly simplified version, but hopefully, you can see where I'm going with the At The Bar exercise. While the above scene is abridged, it reveals what can happen when you employ this exercise. It can be two characters who aren't even in your script. They can be discussing why setting a scene in an empty church might be better for the subtext than setting it in a junkyard. Whatever it is you're struggling with, let your characters help you.

THE MISSION STATEMENT

This one is good for when you just can't get started, or when you've lost your motivation for whatever it is you're working on. Which, by the way, happens to ALL of us.

Write out a mission statement about WHY you want to write this script. You are not allowed to include any sort of loglines, or pitches about what the story is about or who the characters are, or anything else that can be answered with What, Who, Where, or How.

Write the *Why*. Why do you want to write this script? Why do you need to tell this story? Why is now the time for you to write this?

I told you I do this at the start of every project, and it's become an invaluable mechanism to look back on, not only to get me back on track but to also reignite the original fire I had for a particular piece.

BIG NIGHT

This exercise is one I created and named after the amazing 1996 film BIG NIGHT written by Stanley Tucci & Joey Tropiano. Not because the exercise involves food but rather because that film has one of the most brilliantly written scenes in the history of talking cinema and does it without any dialogue. The entire last four minutes and fifty-four seconds of the film do not contain a single word of dialogue. In fact, there are only six words of dialogue spoken in the last six minutes and twenty seconds of the film, yet the ending still manages to bring the entire story and character relationships to an incredibly beautiful and satisfying resolution.

There are three characters in BIG NIGHT's final scene, and despite not a word being spoken, it wraps up the entire movie exactly how it should. It is perfect. Any dialogue would have been superfluous and underestimating the audience. Studio and marketing execs would almost always demand there has to be dialogue. *We HAVE the have them say things to each other!*

Those folks would be wrong.

The BIG NIGHT exercise is to take one of your existing scenes that contain at least two to four characters and write the exact same scene WITHOUT any dialogue.

It doesn't matter what the scene is, where it's set, or how many characters are in it. Just remember not to half-ass it by taking some small scene with only four lines. You must choose a meaty one. Something three to five pages long is perfect. Rewrite the scene as close as you can to your original but sans any dialogue. The length of your Big Night scene does not have to be the same page count—that would be silly. In Tucci & Tropiano's screenplay for BIG NIGHT, that final scene, which is nearly five full minutes long, is only four 8ths of a page in the script. But what you see on screen is exactly what's described on the page.

This is a tremendous exercise for improving your descriptive writing—an element the gurus always try to convince you isn't important—as well as working out your visual storytelling muscles.

Here's the cool bonus part of this exercise: you can do it with other screenwriters' scenes!

Take the scene in JERRY MAGUIRE where Bob Sugar fires Jerry Maguire at the crowded Cronin's Grill. Imagine writing that scene without any dialogue. *WHAT??? Impossible!*

Yes and no. Obviously, there are certain scenes in screenwriting that require dialogue. Duh. You may choose a scene like that. The point of the exercise isn't to create a non-dialogue version that works, though, that would be great, it's just an exercise.

Many more scenes than you think can be written without dialogue. They may not be as good, that's for sure, or they may be much better. But the exercise itself, even when futile, is going to strengthen your writing muscles, and get you into the zone for writing.

Writing begets writing.

So, do it with one of your own genius scenes first. Then try taking a scene with characters talking from one of your favorite films or television series and write the same scene without a spoken word.

You will be amazed by how much fun this exercise is and how much it helps you.

THE TIME TRAVELER

Here's another one that is as much fun as it is helpful. In this one, take a scene—you can do one of your favorites from someone else, but it's always best to take one of your own—and rewrite it set in a different time and place.

Say you have a scene with two criminals discussing how to rob a bank in current-day Chicago. Take that scene and rewrite it with those same thieves but now it's in Madrid in 1957. They're still discussing robbing a bank, but let's see how much atmosphere and tone you can bring to a completely different time and space.

The opposite works just as well. If you have a story with two shepherds set in the 19th-century Scottish Highlands, rewrite it with those same characters talking about the same subject matter, but now it's set today and they're a pair of workers at the Bronx Zoo.

If your story takes place on a spaceship in the year 2455, rewrite it so it's on a train in 1870 Texas.

The key is to make sure the scene ends up giving the same emotion, character reveal, and information as the original.

Ah, but don't forget—your characters' speech and mannerisms change. How will their language and responses and awareness change? Remember, you want to write the exact same characters but different versions of themselves. Don't have the Scottish shepherds talking and acting like 19th-century shepherds in modern-day New York. You need to write them as who they'd be in this new time.

The Time Traveler exercise really helps open your imagination when it comes to the characters you populate your writing with. I was stuck on a period piece I wrote once. It was set in Missouri during the early 1920s. There were a couple of scenes that I just couldn't get right. Version after version, draft after draft, it just wasn't quite there.

So, I did the Time Traveler exercise. I took the characters and that same scene and set it in current-day Tijuana. Wow! At first, it was awful (be prepared for that), but the more I really put some effort into trying to write a quality scene, the better it got. Before I was done with my second draft of the time traveler scene, I had figured out a solution to my original period piece. I went back in and voila! Improvement. Momentum. Inspiration.

WRITING WITHOUT WRITING

This section could have gone in the process chapter, but I have a non-writing exercise to share, so I dropped it here. Writing without writing is also one of the ways I write. It's not procrastination. Again, you need self-awareness to be at your best in this endeavor. Writing without writing means when we're working but we are not actually typing. Or doing research, or anything consciously connected to our script.

But we're working.

To paraphrase Burton Rascoe, "*What no spouse of a writer will ever understand is that when the writer is sitting in a chair staring out the window, they are actually working.*"

I will write without writing when I'm on my bike, on the golf course, or cooking. Again, this isn't procrastination, I'm not avoiding the work. It's when I need to figure something out that isn't coming from sitting at the keyboard. So, I do something creative that is not writing. I don't sit in front of the TV flipping channels or scroll social media. I do something that engages my creative right brain without focusing on whatever writer problem I need to solve. Cycling is creative for me. The way I ride, where I ride, etc. Golf is creative. Cooking is very creative. Writing without writing is a great way to solve script issues.

Okay, so the exercise . . . warning: this one takes a few hours, so make time.

Choose a movie or television episode that is somehow similar to whatever you're working on. If you're writing a rom-com, choose a rom-com. If you're writing a Western, choose something that has classic Western themes if not an actual Western. We're not looking for copycat stuff here, we're just looking for something in a similar genre or world.

Get a copy of the screenplay: an actual copy, not one of those terrible transcriptions the internet is littered with. Get the script and read it all the way through. Not as a writer, but as a reader. Read the script from beginning to end, then take a break. Grab some food, return emails, whatever. Then . . .

Watch the film or episode. And watch it with the script open in front of you. Follow along page by page. See what dialogue changed, what locations are different. Note how the editing changed the order of some scenes, what characters might be gone or new ones who aren't in the script. See how the ending lands compared to how it did for the read.

This is a Masterclass in learning how all the stuff we've been talking about that affects the final product. How and why things change. How the language and description on the page is interpreted by the director and actors and cinematographers. How the tiniest changes in a location or setting can alter the story.

This is a great screenwriting exercise, and a great filmmaking one, too.

THE PLAGIARIST

This one was a big favorite years ago, then lost its shine for whatever reason. But it's still one the very best screenwriting exercises for newer, less experienced writers. Like writing without writing, get yourself a script from a film or episode of television you like. Open it up next to your computer screen and literally type the script. Word for word, ellipsis for ellipsis. Exactly as written.

Doing this will give you the *feeling* of telling a story at a level above where you are. YELLOWJACKETS, MOONLIGHT, KNIVES OUT, TED LASSO, any script you want. As you retype that screenwriter's story a magical thing happens . . . you will *feel* the story. You will sense the characters and their relationships, the connection between setting and tone, and the emotional impact of the dialogue and description. I know it sounds kooky, but it's true. It's an incredible experience.

When you go back to your own work after this exercise, you will first feel incredibly inspired and like you're better than you've ever been . . . and then you'll feel like a complete fraud. That's okay, it's part of the gig.

Those are the best exercises I know. Give them a shot and let me know if they helped.

13

TRUE HOLLYWOOD TALES

NO BOOK BY someone who's spent years inside the Hollywood machine would be complete without some tales from the trenches. What follows are just a few of the experiences I've had throughout my career.

THE BEST NOTE I EVER RECEIVED

The best note, and by best, I mean most outrageous I ever received in my screenwriting career (to date) was from my second staff job. After my terrible year on FELICITY, I took a job with a show called LEVEL 9, on the now-defunct UPN network. The show was ahead of its time in it was about cyber cops chasing cyber criminals through cyberspace.

If a current version was pitched today, it would likely find an audience. But this was back when the coolest thing on the Internet was Ask Jeeves! No social media, there wasn't even Facebook or YouTube yet. But there we were, doing a show about cyberspace.

The show aired between SHASTA MCNASTY and HOMEBOYS IN OUTER SPACE, a spot as metaphorical as it was literal.

The network was desperate to capture the 18–24 audience demographic, but unfortunately, those in charge of trying to figure out what young viewers wanted were a bunch of old white men. I was tasked with writing an episode about digital art being used to create fakes of famous paintings. Bad guys were using the technology no one had heard of at the time to create perfect copies of works by van Gogh and other artists to sell for millions. Time for the cops of LEVEL 9 to stop these shenanigans!

My episode, like the series itself, had little to no gunplay, little violence, and no blood. Our cops used their brains to catch bad guys. I turned my episode in to the studio and waited for notes. Back then people used fax machines (look it up) for cutting edge communication. Since the writers' offices were located about twelve miles from the studio (that's 6000 miles in LA traffic terms), the studio would fax their notes to us. The writers would hear the fax machine kick in, and we'd all gather to see if our scripts were liked or hated, and how much we were going to have to rewrite.

For whatever reason when the notes on my episode came in, they were not from whatever midlevel exec covered our show and usually sent the notes; this was from the head of the studio himself. Holy Overall Deal, Batman! This was either a great sign for me, or the carving on my writer headstone.

Our showrunner was out that day, but the rest of the writing staff gathered in the supervising producer's office because he had the fax machine. I could see the notes were very short, just a few lines. GREAT! The head of the studio only had a single note on my script!

> *Great script! Love the art stuff! One thought we'd like you to address: Can you put a severed head in the teaser? Because according to our research kids dig severed heads!*

We all stared at each other.

Huh?

The head of the studio wanted a severed head in the opening three minutes of my episode of a show with almost no blood or violence because *according to their research*, kids dig severed heads???

Once the fax had been passed around, we did what any good writing staff would do.

We laughed our asses off.

It was the most ridiculous and insane thing any of us had ever seen.

One of the writers ended up framing the fax and hanging it in their office.

When the showrunner returned, he had little reaction beyond rolling his eyes. He was a grizzled veteran of more than thirty years in the biz, and I guess nothing blipped his radar anymore.

He told me he'd handle the rewrite. I never saw my script again until it was time to head up to Vancouver to shoot the episode. I read it on the plane.

No severed head.

The show was canceled after only thirteen episodes. Clearly the head of the studio knew something we didn't.

THE HELICOPTER NOTE

I met with some producers at Sony Television once and pitched them an idea for a series. They loved it. Bought it in the room and paid me to write the pilot. No going out and pitching, they believed in this idea and the power of the story.

It was a cop show set in St. Louis, Missouri. It had a very cool modern day Miami Vice type of vibe.

When I turned in my first draft, I went down to the Sony lot and met with the producer, his development exec, and his assistant. We all sat in the producer's office, and he gave me his thoughts on my script, and the other two people did what I call the **notes nod**—a physical phenomenon that strikes lower-level execs whenever an upper-level exec says *anything*.

When he was done, he turned to his development person and his assistant and asked them if they had anything to add. They both gave their notes.

The assistant and development person gave notes that were innocuous, just a regurgitation of the producer's, and I went off to do my rewrite. A week later I turned in my second draft and found myself back in the same office with the same people for round two of notes on what was known as the *Untitled Paul Guyot Project.*

This time the notes were a little different.

The producer gave his thoughts, the other two did the *notes nod*, and then he turned it over to them. His assistant spoke up first, repeating exactly what the producer had said, just using different words. Then it was the development executive's turn. What follows is a transcript as close to verbatim as I can recall . . .

DE: Did you see *24* last night?

ME: Uh, no, I did not.

DE: Well, last night, Jack Bauer was hanging off a helicopter and it was just super cool . . . you didn't see it?

ME: I did not.

ASSISTANT: It was super cool.

DE: So cool, right?

ME: Okay.

DE: I'm just watching this like everyone else in the country and like everyone else I'm just thinking this is super cool.

(*I glance at the producer—he's stone-faced*)

ME: Sounds . . . cool.

DE: Super cool. And then as I'm getting my coffee this morning, I'm thinking you know what? You should put a helicopter in your script.

(I wait for more but nothing comes.)

ME: Okay . . . is there a particular scene you're thinking about or situation?

DE: I don't know, it's just, you know, the helicopter thing is super cool, and putting one in the pilot would just make it so . . .

ME: Cool?

DE: Yes!

(*all three do the notes nod)*

ME: All right. I will . . . take a look at that.

I leave Sony, completely forgetting the helicopter discussion by the time I get to Tito's Tacos. Everyone who has a meeting at Sony goes to Tito's Tacos afterward. First, it's practically across the street, and second, it's a California state law.

Over the next few days, I do my pass and turn in the script. The following week I am back in the office. Everyone loves the script. The producer says things like, "*We are really close here!*" and starts talking about casting and directors. The assistant is so excited he doesn't even bother changing his words when he parrots what his boss said.

Then the development executive speaks up . . . "*Where's the helicopter?*"

"*The what?*"

She reminds me of our last notes meeting where I "agreed" (her word) to put a helicopter in the script. I'm stunned. I look to the producer for help. He's Mount Rushmore.

I look back at the development exec, scrambling to save myself. I babble something like, "*Uh, I couldn't really find a place where it seemed to fit organically into the story.*" Her reply is something along the lines of, "*Well, I'm not a writer, but . . .*"

They LOVE to say, "*I'm not a writer, but . . .*" and then give you notes on your writing.

She tells me she's not a writer, says being organic isn't always important, then gives me a final reminder that "*A helicopter would be super cool.*"

Now it's time for me to do the notes nod.

I drive back home in a fog. *Put a helicopter in the script because they're super cool . . .*

I go through every scene in the script, every situation, and there is no place for a helicopter, cool or not. So, I decide to try something.

My script opens with the sun rising over the glistening St. Louis Arch. Everyone had loved my opening from the first draft on. Here's how I rewrote it to service her note . . .

```
EXT. SAINT LOUIS - DAY

The sun is just rising, its rays reflect off the 630-
foot GATEWAY ARCH, the tallest man-made monument in
the Western Hemisphere, giving the city a surreal
gloaming.

A helicopter screams through frame.
```

That's it. That's all I did. We never see the helicopter again anywhere in the script. I turn in the script and wait. Four days later I was back in the office.

The development executive LOVED the script! She never mentioned the helicopter again and neither did anyone else.

THE DARK

After JUDGING AMY my then wife wanted to move back to Saint Louis to raise our family. I figured my screenwriting career was over, and I would teach or write the great American novel . . . or the mediocre American novel. God had other plans. We hadn't even closed on our Midwest house when my agent at the time called to say Stephen J. Cannell had read a script of mine and wanted to talk with me. Turns out we were both at CAA, and his agent told my agent he was looking for a young writer to work with on a pilot. He had been writing novels the last few years, and this was to be his big comeback into television.

I was a huge fan of Cannell's work, from THE ROCKFORD FILES to WISEGUY, and was in complete fanboy mode when the phone rang and the person on the other end said, "I have Steve Cannell calling for you."

On that call, Cannell gave me what is still today probably the best compliment I've ever received about my writing: *"You write with knuckles, kid."*

My insecure self momentarily assumed he meant either there were so many typos, or my script was so bad it was as if I didn't even know how to type.

Luckily, he continued before I said anything, telling me how my writing was raw and honest, original and authentic.

Knuckles.

He hired me over the phone, saying he had an idea for a series, but wanted me to write it; I would get the Created By credit. He would be an Executive Producer on it, and we would work together with him supervising me and my writing.

This led to a great working relationship and ultimately a treasured friendship. Cannell and I spent a lot of time together over the next few months. I will always cherish how he took me in, bringing me into his world, from working on the script at his Laguna home, to those lunch "meetings" inside Musso & Frank, sitting in his personal booth, watching him eat tuna on white with extra mayo.

The studio was Warner Brothers and Peter Roth was the head of it at the time. He and Cannell went way back so he was personally overseeing this project. It was for the TNT network, and Warner Brothers was going to guide us through the process to make sure we delivered exactly what the network wanted.

The studio loved the title—THE DARK—because the network wanted dark. "*Go darker, go darker,*" is what we kept hearing during our notes calls.

So we did. I wrote something very dark, and thanks to Cannell's help, very cool. The studio loved the script and paid to shoot it. We hired Walter Hill to direct. This was amazing for me because before I became a paid screenwriter, I spent many years as a Stand-in. I worked on a couple of Walter's films, and he and I became friends. Walter knew I was an aspiring screenwriter and was always generous with his time and advice. The fact he was directing my first pilot to be shot was a full circle moment I can't put into words.

We had an incredible cast consisting of Colleen Porch, Erik Jensen, Fred Ward, and Billy Burke. To this day, this cast was the best I've ever worked with. Walter did his usual great job of directing and when we screened it for Peter Roth, he dubbed it, *"Perfect!"* Dark and creepy and very cool! We had a hit on our hands!

Then the network saw it.

And the TNT executives said, and I quote, *"We can't put this on the air. It's too dark."*

Hollywood is a verb.

I got Hollywooded.

HOW I BECAME A PROFESSIONAL SCREENWRITER

The last non-writing job I ever held in my life was assistant to the great Hong Kong actor, Chow Yun-Fat. I was blessed to be his first-ever American born assistant, and being a giant fan of HK cinema, this was a bucket list type of dream.

He was doing THE REPLACEMENT KILLERS, his first American studio production, and for over five months I spent nearly every day with him and his amazing wife, Jasmine, who only referred to me as "Fe Lung," (Fat Dragon) as I was a bit on the chunky side back then.

I helped them find their LA apartment for the shoot, I went shopping with them, to breakfast and dinner, and pretty much drove Yun-Fat anywhere he had to go.

Walking through LA's Chinatown with him one Saturday morning was an incredible experience. It must have been like being around the Beatles in the 60s. He was mob everywhere, and what should have been a twenty-minute excursion to buy some treats for Jasmine, turned into a two-hour festival of love. Yun-Fat smiled for every picture, signed every autograph, made sure every single person was personally greeted and felt like they were the only one there. When we were finally able to leave, I asked him something like, "*Don't you ever lose your patience with all those people?*" Yun-Fat smiled that luminous grin of his and said, "*No. I owe them everything. Without them, I am nothing.*"

There's a few American celebrities who could learn from Yun-Fat.

So, what does this gig have to do with how I became a professional screenwriter? Yun-Fat and I became good friends. He loved that I knew about HK cinema and all his previous work. We talked about screenwriting in Hong Kong vs. America, we talked about the books we loved, and the writers we admired. He knew I wanted to be a screenwriter and that I had spent years working as a Stand-in while writing my little scripts. As we were wrapping up THE REPLACEMENT KILLERS and prepping to go to New York to shoot THE CORRUPTOR, Yun-Fat invited me on a walk one day. We walked for a while in silence, something that was not uncommon, and then he asked me how my writing was going. I gave him my pat answer; some version of, "Going great, hard to find time to write, blah, blah, blah." We walked some more. Silence. Then he said, "*When people ask me how to become an actor, you know what I tell them? I tell them: start acting.*"

He stopped and stared at me with that grin. I nodded dumbly, and then he leaned in and very quietly said, "*If you come to New York with us and continue being an assistant, I will fire you.*"

Then he put his arm around me, and we walked on.

I did not go to New York with him. Six months later I got my first paid screenwriting gig.

FELICITY

When I was hired by JJ Abrams for my very first staff position, I was thrilled. Not just to get my break but to have it be on what was one of the hot shows in television, and to be working with someone as talented as JJ. This was just before he became a household name, but everyone in Hollywood knew him. He was an amazing writer, and had just signed a huge deal at Disney.

He hired me during my meeting/interview inside a hotel room at the Chateau Marmont, the infamous auberge on the Sunset Strip. What was crazy was the show had just begun production on season two, and JJ wanted me to go immediately to the writers room at the Felicity offices. At the time I had no idea how crazy this was because

I had no frame of reference. I dutifully hopped into my car and made the 45-minute drive to my first official staff job!

When I walked into the writers room there were only three other writers in there, and they stared at me like I was an alien. I told them I was the new writer, and let's just say that news didn't go over well. I explained JJ had literally just hired me an hour ago at the Chateau Marmont and told me to come down here. They asked what shows I had written on. I said this was my first. They all looked at each other. I had been there all of five minutes and you would have needed a chainsaw to cut the tension.

I took a seat and they continued what they had been doing before I arrived; trying to break story. While this was the first writers room I was in as an actual staff member, I had been around the SNOOPS room multiple times. That show, created by David E. Kelley, had a staff of seasoned professionals, and just from the four or five days I spent around them, I could tell this FELICITY room was populated by writers who—comparatively speaking—had no idea what they were doing. Or if they did, their attitudes were so sour and full of acrimony, it kept them from doing any quality work.

I made the mistake of opening my mouth once, not to pitch anything mind you, just to ask a question, and the scorn thrown back at me kept me quiet for the remaining two hours.

When they finally called it, having done nothing but put a single card up on the board, two of the writers filed out immediately. The senior writer stayed behind, doing that thing where a person fakes stacking papers. I figured she wanted to talk, so I told her I was very excited to be there and learn all I could.

With that, she leaned across the table and said, "*You need to understand something. We don't want you here. None of us do. JJ only hired you to spite us because we wanted a friend of ours for the job. So, just know that you don't matter. The best thing you can do is stay out of our way.*"

And she walked out of the office.

Welcome to Hollywood, Guyot.

Unfortunately, that day was one of the better days I had on the show. Over the course of that season, these three writers made a focused effort to keep me feeling as unwanted and as much of an outsider as possible. If they had only worked this hard on breaking story.

These three—grown adults, mind you—would do things such as: say we were all meeting in a certain writer's office and then as I followed them in, they'd shut the door in my face. Or they'd tell me we were all going to lunch at 12:30, and when I came out of my office at 12:15 the PA tells me they went to lunch at noon. Or if I opened my mouth in the room to pitch something, or to *yes, and* someone's idea, literally anytime I spoke up, I was met with one of two reactions. Either they would stare at me in complete silence, or they would tell me whatever I said was wrong or stupid (or both), making sure to add something along the lines of, *"That's not how it's done."* One morning I entered my office to find a bottle of water spilled across my desk . . . a bottle of water that wasn't there when I left the night before.

It was all high school level bullshit (barely), and just showed how insecure and terrified the three of them were. Unfortunately, for me and the show itself, JJ wasn't around much that season. He was developing ALIAS at the time, and doing other things connected to his new Disney deal. A typical week was the four writers in the room trying to break story, then JJ popping in once or twice a week, looking at what we all had, and saying no to most of it. Then he'd leave and we would have to start all over again.

The three writers took great offense to this, but the thing was, JJ was right. Their work sucked. But they were far too down the rabbit hole of hating on him to see it.

I'm not exaggerating when I say most days that season were spent sitting around the writers room while the three of them complained about JJ. Talked about how much they *hated* him, how much they *hated* the show. And here's what made it even worse.

Whenever JJ would show up, these three kissed his ass like he was a king. I marveled at how seamlessly and quickly they could go from spewing hatred toward him to being sycophants of the highest order in his presence.

It made me physically ill.

The show wasn't that difficult to write. JJ had created some great characters, and we had all lived through college life. But if you listened to these three, you'd think we were trying to break story for some complex international spy thriller with a dozen series regulars, a locked room mystery, and a cliffhanger in each episode.

I was so depressed after only a few weeks I called my agent and told him I wanted to quit. He said I can't quit. He said if I quit my very first job as a television writer, no one would ever hire me again. He said I needed to do whatever it took to survive.

Survive and advance. Just make it to the end of the season.

Okay. I mentally worked out how best to survive the remaining seven or eight months. And let me tell you, what I thought was the best way to do it was one of the many, many mistakes I've made in my career. My plan was terrible, disastrous. What was it?

I decided I would do everything I could to gain acceptance from the other writers. Since I was with them more than anyone else, I would put all my effort into getting them to like me, or at least accept me.

Like I said, terrible plan.

Instead of bearing down and trying to be the best working professional screenwriter I could be, the self-loathing damaged person I was decided, forget that! Just make them like you!

Ugh.

You would think after seeing me five days a week, month in and month out, and me now being as sugary sweet as I could be, there might be some sort of letdown in their rage and childish attitudes.

Nope.

If anything, it increased. After I turned in my first episode, JJ came into my office to personally tell me what a great job I did. That made me feel excellent. But no sooner did he say that when he was off to other places again, and I was left with the three trolls.

Leaving my office after JJ giving me kudos, I was excited to tell the other three. I thought if they knew JJ liked my writing, they will like me! Can you see how damaged I was?

I asked the office PA where the other writers were, and he pointed to one of their offices which had its door closed.

I was about to knock when I heard them inside. They were reading aloud from my script and laughing. They were making jokes about it. I stood outside the door for at least a couple of minutes listening to my dialogue and description being mocked before heading back to my own office and closing the door.

Survive and advance.

As we rolled into the "back nine" of the season—that's the last nine episodes of a (usually) twenty-two-episode order— things were still the same. I loved being on set. The actors and crew on FELICITY were fabulous. JJ Abrams and Matt Reeves were great. Unfortunately, 90% of my time on the show was spent with the other three writers.

One day when the three were being particularly treacherous to me, I thought I was going to have a breakdown. It was the nadir of my season, and I decided enough was enough. I walked out of the writers room without a word and went straight into the office of JJ's partner, Matt Reeves. Matt was the Co-Creator and handled all the directing and cinematic aspects of the show while JJ focused on the writing. Matt was someone who hated confrontation, and he was smart enough to feel the tension around the writers' offices, so he did his best to be invisible.

Matt was a cheerful, caring guy and gave me a big smile when I walked in and asked what was up . . .

And I started to cry. Sob is more accurate.

Through my sobs, I told him I couldn't take it anymore. I couldn't handle all the toxicity and disrespect and just plain meanness of the writing staff. He had to do something!

Matt stared at me with bewilderment. I stood there wiping my eyes and sniffling. Then Matt Reeves said something that changed my life, not just as a screenwriter, but as a man, as a human being.

Matt said, "*I'm sorry, I can't help you.*"

There was about two full seconds of absolute humiliation as I was suddenly outside my body looking at myself standing there whining like a toddler, and then a light went off in my head. Not just a light, but an SX-16 Nightsun.

Matt Reeves was right. He couldn't help me. No one was coming to save me. I had to get up off the floor and save myself. Still one of the greatest life lessons.

As much as the three writers were acting like spoiled, insecure, cruel fourteen-year-olds, I wasn't being any more mature by letting all their actions get to me. To paraphrase Richard Bach: *"If your happiness depends on the behavior of other people, then you're the one with the problem."*

It wasn't the trolls' fault. They were being who they were. They were all going through their own hell. I've yet to meet a mean person who was happy. They might project happiness and contentment, but it's not authentic. In my experience, when people have an anger issue, it's usually a pain issue. But I never understood this until after that day when Matt Reeves delivered the most aesthetically exquisite kick in the balls in the history of the modern American television writer.

During that time in my life, I was just as insecure and self-loathing as those three writers. My pain just manifested differently. I did not take it out on others. I turned it inward. I'd had a horrible upbringing, married the wrong person for the wrong reasons—though, God blessed us with the most amazing children ever—and had a habit of eating my feelings late at night, my feelings usually buried deep inside a party-size bag of Wavy Lay's potato chips. Thus, what had been happening inside the Felicity offices was like dumping acetone on a fire.

But Matt's six words that day changed everything. For the final months of that season, I was a different person. No longer was I trying to gain the approval of the other writers or prove my worth to them. No longer was I feeling less of a person because of their words and actions.

I started speaking up in the room, no longer sugar-coating my opinion of their shoddy work, and began to offer better solutions to story issues. I knew I was a good writer, every bit as good and probably better than any of them, and finally began to do the job I was hired for—being a working professional screenwriter.

At one point when they tried the old "shut the door in the kid's face" gag, I slammed my palm into it so hard the door nearly came off the hinges. They never tried it again.

One day when we were fortunate enough to have JJ in the room all day, he turned to me at one point and said, "*What happened to you? You barely speak for eight months, now you're the funniest, most confident guy in the room.*"

When that season of FELICITY came to an end, my agent called with good news; JJ and Matt wanted me back for the next season. I declined. My agent was extremely disappointed, but to his credit he understood. He didn't try to talk me into staying, he just went out and found me another job. And I got the meeting and subsequent offer because I had worked an *entire season* on one of the most popular shows on TV.

Survive and advance.

The careers of those three writers took interesting avenues. Over the next several years one of them continued to kiss JJ's ass, following him onto other shows, no doubt speaking ill of him and his family unless the man himself was in the room. Another one was fired from several jobs; I guess the old shut the door thing didn't go over so well with other writers. The third writer—the one who had warned me to stay out of their way that first day—almost never worked again.

Me? In the ensuing years since surviving that season in Hell, the longest I've ever gone without a paid screenwriting gig is ten months, and that was by choice.

Call it karma. Call it God. Call it whatever you want. I prefer to think of it in terms of what my friend and former boss, Hart Hanson used to say. Hart had this wonderful theory that no matter what . . . bad people always come together. Bad people always crash into other bad people.

14

HOW TO SPOT A SCREENWRITING FRAUD

I HAVE TALKED a lot about the frauds out there, and how important it is to avoid them. The gurus, the charlatans, the conmen, the poseurs. Most of the time it's obvious who they are. But there are some out there spewing their lies and bad advice while wearing full camouflage.

How do we spot them?

Do not fear, I am here to reveal the weasels in owl's clothing . . .

Most of the screenwriting websites claim to have "screenwriting experts" readily available to judge your work and your talent, to give you authoritative instruction, to share the secrets of how to become the next QT or Shonda. At first glance, some of these so-called experts sound like the real deal. Some even have links to their IMDb page with their plethora of credits as proof of their expertise.

Here's some more truth: anyone can put anything on IMDb. Even on IMDb Pro. They just have to pay before they inflate their resumes or outright lie. I've seen IMDb Pro pages belonging to writer's assistants who have listed themselves as executive producers and showrunners on series they weren't even affiliated with.

So, how are we supposed to tell who's legit and who's full of it? It's easier than you think.

The first and easiest way to spot a screenwriting fraud is when their credits and/or experience is non-specific. They love the non-specific proof of excellence. The best way I can show you this is by sharing ACTUAL examples from the Bio and About pages of screenwriting sites that are charging you money for their expert opinion of you and your work.

Here's one that sounds impressive:

» *RECOGNIZED AS AN EXPERT IN THE SCREENWRITING WORLD*

Really? By whom? I've spent more than half my life in the Screenwriting World, and I've never heard of this person. Nor have any of my fellow working professional screenwriters.

I recognize Aaron Sorkin and Randi Mayem Singer and John Ridley as experts in the Screenwriting World, but this person? Never heard of them. Ever. Perhaps it's because this person has zero credits, and nothing to show what qualifies them as a recognized expert, or if they even know the first thing about screenwriting.

» *WORKS WITH SOME OF THE TOP PRODUCERS IN THE INDUSTRY*

Oh, boy! This person MUST be legit! I mean, they work with some of the TOP producers in the industry! They must work with Jason Blum and Dede Gardner and Dan Lin and Megan Ellison and and and . . .

Only thing is, you don't see this person's name anywhere but their own site. Not on any projects by top producers or even lousy producers. Not in the Trades, not even on the capricious IMDb. Perhaps they're a security guard at the gate into the neighborhood where the top producers live? Or maybe they walk top producers' dogs?

» HAS RELATIONSHIPS WITH OVER 60 MAJOR PRODUCTION COMPANIES

Really? What type of relationship? Is it our dog walker again? Or could it be an assistant at a marketing company that has "relationships" with production companies? Or a barista at a coffee joint where production companies place large orders? And sixty? Really? I don't think even Craig Mazin or Scott Frank have that many relationships. Are there even sixty major production companies? I counted all the major production companies I know of here and abroad and came up with . . . thirty-three. But I'm not that familiar with the film industry of the Solomon Islands.

You may think I'm being facetious or worse here. I am not.

If these people don't tell you WHO they work with and in WHAT capacity; if they don't tell you what TYPE of relationship they have and NAME the production companies, how are we to trust them?

» WRITES FOR PRODUCERS AND DIRECTORS AROUND THE WORLD

Hmm, this sounds like it has possibilities, right? I mean, at least they're a writer. And they write for producers and directors around the world!

But, umm, what producers? What directors? Doing a deep dive, I find nothing with their name on it anywhere. Perhaps they write dry cleaning receipts? Or parking tickets in Burbank or Cape Town? If they won't name these global producers and directors, how do we know if it's at best fudging the truth, or at worst, an outright lie?

>> *AWARD-WINNING SCREENWRITER*

This tell is similar to what happens in the book world. Have you ever noticed that every single author you meet, or see on Facebook or anywhere else is a "bestselling" author? How can that be, right? Every author can't be a BEST seller. Then there would be nobody to outsell.

The way they get away with saying this is twofold.

1. Some folks just lie. It sucks, but it's true. Not many, but some.
2. They call themselves a bestseller even if the mise en scene in which they did their "best" selling is, shall we say, a tad limited?

An author can call themselves a bestseller if their book sold "best" in any sort of sub-category of a sub-genre of a sub-genre's sub-category.

- Romance Thrillers set inside a nunnery with protagonists between the ages of thirty-five and thirty-seven who have dual citizenship and speak with Turkish accents.
- Cozy mysteries set in towns of less than 2500 but more than 1000, located no more than three kilometers from a tectonic estuary where a minimum of 18% of the population have no hands.

Get the picture?

When it comes to the film and TV industry, or rather the perimeter around it, I think there are more folks calling themselves "award-winning" than there have been awards given out. Ever. Here's the thing to remember when you see this: if they don't TELL YOU what awards they've won, chances are very good they are lying, because having a certificate printed up and framed by your grandmother that reads *Best Writer Ever!* doesn't really count. If they're not lying, then they're misleading you. I've seen many folks call themselves an "Emmy-winning writer" when the truth is they worked in some non-writing capacity on some news program that won some regional Emmy award. Yes, technically, they "won" an Emmy, but they know they're embellishing the truth.

Next is one of my favorites . . .

>> OUR SCRIPT CONSULTANTS HAVE SIGNIFICANT INDUSTRY CREDITS.

I am laughing right now. What are these significant credits? IF they are truly *significant*, why would they not be listed? If you want to convince people of your expertise and you have *significant* industry credits, wouldn't you list them? Don't you want to prove you are in fact what you claim to be? By the way, to learn the TRUTH about "script consultants" check out the glossary chapter of this book.

If a person won't tell you what their credits are, run. If they say something like, they'd tell you, but they can't due to an NDA, or because some evil entity refused to give them credit, run faster.

Another way to spot a screenwriting fraud is when you see the word READER.

Run. Run fast. Run to the nearest train and get on it regardless of where it's going.

You probably hear as much about "readers" from the gurus and charlatans as you do about "structure." And they're just as wrong, if not more so, when it comes to readers.

Here's the truth about Hollywood readers . . .

The whole reader thing kicked off in the 1980s when script sales were first reported by the Trades. Before they started telling the world about the seven figure deals Shane Black and Joe Eszterhas were getting for their spec scripts, no one really knew screenwriters could get rich.

Prior to the '80s, scripts were read by lower-level studio execs, secretaries (sic), and the like. Once the public got wind that there was gold in them thar hills, everyone and their dog walker came to Hollywood with screenplays in hand. Studios and producers were overwhelmed with scripts and thus, employed readers—people whose job it was to do nothing more than read.

Hence the name.

The rise of the reader being a direct connection to the rise of spec script sales is why the books and gurus began all the hype about readers. Readers were the first "gatekeepers" of Hollywood. Suddenly, readers had power, though it was rice paper thin. Suddenly, being a reader was an easy way to get into the Hollywood parties, to be seen as a player. If you were failing at screenwriting, become a reader, then you can judge of all those asshats who write better than you!

At the height of this madness, readers would take home as many as twenty scripts over a weekend, read them, and do what is called "Coverage."

Coverage lists the screenplay's qualities or drawbacks (in the reader's opinion), gives a brief synopsis of the story, and then drops one of three opinions:

RECOMMEND—the reader recommends the producer or studio read this script with an eye toward buying it.

CONSIDER—the reader recommends the producer/studio "consider" reading the script. Duh.

PASS—the reader suggests there is no reason for anyone to waste their time with the script.

Readers were paid per script. I knew some readers back in the 90s who worked for Joel Silver's Silver Pictures and were paid as much as $75 per script. I also know of readers at smaller companies or working for independent producers who were paid as little as $25 per read. There was no standard.

And yes, what you're probably thinking right now is true . . . there might have been the greatest screenplay in the history of cinema written during this time that some idiot reader passed on, which caused that writer to give up, and now she's working at a dollar store in Egg Harbor. Not likely, but possible. Maybe likely.

The ultimate horror story of readers is this . . . I once lived with a dude back in the day. We were both aspiring screenwriters. I was working as a Stand-in, and he was working as a reader at a big-time production company located on the Paramount lot. He would bring home these scripts—as many as they would let him; the more scripts, the more money—and if he read a script that was really good, like just blew him away, he would give it a Pass, or a begrudging Consider. Never a Recommend.

Why? Because he was so jealous and insecure when it came to other screenwriters, he couldn't help himself. He felt like he was eliminating his competition by passing on good scripts. While I'm sure this was not the norm at all, it does show one of the many flaws of the whole reader idea.

Here's the current lie regarding these Hollywood readers . . . in the last ten years or so, the majority of studios and legit production companies have done away with readers. The industry isn't as saturated with scripts as it was back then—most of the non-professional scripts have filtered to contests and websites and such.

Most folks who read scripts today are assistants working for agents and producers. Lower-level executives do a lot of reading of potential content. It's gone back to the way it was for the most part. This isn't out of any altruistic move by the powers that be, but rather because they realized, *"Hey, why pay readers who likely know nothing about screenwriting when we can have our employees (who hopefully know a little more) read scripts!"*

So, when you hear the gurus shouting about the notorious gatekeepers of Hollywood known as "The Readers" and how you must pay said guru to get the secrets in order to get beyond the readers, run.

Where most coverage exists today is at agencies and management companies—reading submissions by potential clients, but again, those "readers" aren't readers, they're assistants, and reading is just one of their many duties.

Back to spotting frauds. When you see these sites claiming they have "Professional readers" working for them, remember the qualifications required to be a reader. I will list all of them here:

1. The ability to read.
2. Nope, there is no 2.

That's it. That is literally all one needs. No experience as a writer, no understanding of story or character, or cinema, nothing other than the ability to read.

Here are more actual excerpts from screenwriting websites describing why you should give them your money . . .

» *ALL OUR READERS HAVE INDUSTRY EXPERIENCE AT AGENCIES, STUDIOS, AND FOREIGN SALES FIRMS*

All right, let's all say it together: *They know how to read.*

» *WRITTEN COVERAGE FOR COMPANIES AND STUDIOS INCLUDING PARAMOUNT, WB, AND MANY MORE*

This one at least lists names of actual studios, so one might think, "*Ooo, they MUST know what they're doing if Paramount or WB trusted them to read!*"

No.

Go back to my story about my former roommate who read for that very same Paramount. Just because someone was employed by a major studio does not mean they know the first thing about screenwriting, or how to know what is good or bad writing.

A cousin to The Reader is the person who just reads or watches . . .

>> *HAVE READ HUNDREDS OF SCRIPTS/WATCHED HUNDREDS OF MOVIES*

This is one you see a lot on social media. It's also the only qualification listed by a very well-known self-proclaimed "Story Expert" (WTF?) who's written multiple books on screenwriting but never penned one screenplay himself.

People offering advice, some even charging you money, and they tell you the reason they're qualified to give you THE WRITER advice is because they've read lots of scripts or watched lots of movies? Well, I've watched thousands of hours of Formula 1 racing, but I'm self-aware enough to know that gives me no informed opinion whatsoever in giving someone advice on how to be an F1 driver.

If the person isn't a working professional screenwriter, WHY would you ever trust anything they tell you about how to become a working professional screenwriter?

This leads me to another type of fraud:

>> *THE EXCITED NEWBIE*

Social media is stuffed with people who are clearly in the embryonic stage of their own screenwriting careers, but because they've written ONE script, or made ONE short film, and have big plans for their own future, they feel qualified to give you notes and advice. Again, let's equate.

That would be like me making spaghetti and meatballs ONE TIME, using store-bought dry pasta and the grocery's pre-made meatballs, and then going onto social media to tell you how to cook like Missy Robbins.

I don't get angry at these frauds, though. I just feel sorry for them. They are on a desperate quest for validation and relevance, and thus, they self-image actualize to feel seen.

The next way to spot a screenwriting fraud is probably my favorite of them all, and I have to give these folks their flowers because they're not lying!

I found some websites offering "professional" screenwriting services for a price where the folks taking your money and giving that *professional* advice have no experience whatsoever with screenwriting or any other aspect of our industry. But they're not lying! In their bios, they proudly tell you they have zero experience with anything connected to Hollywood, yet they want you to trust their opinion of your work. Here are my two favorites:

» *COMES FROM A SUCCESSFUL BACKGROUND IN CORPORATE TRAINING*

Yep. This cat never even tried to be a screenwriter. Never participated in any of the screenwriter-adjacent vocations we've discussed. He just saw an opportunity to make money off folks desperate to break in to Hollywood. He has taken his corporate training experience and applied it to judging your ability as a screenwriter. Gotta love this dude! But I love this next person even more.

» *PREVIOUSLY WORKED AS A VP ACCOUNTANT AT MOTOROLA, MCDONALD'S, AND OTHER LARGE COMPANIES*

Amazing. A corporate accountant has decided to charge you money to tell you what is right and wrong with your screenplay. If I wanted to throw my money away, I would go to this person long before I'd go to a "reader" or any of the other frauds!

Remember, I am not making these up. At the time of this writing, they are all right there online for you to see.

Lastly, I found a site offering all sorts of screenwriting services and instruction from their *"Faculty of industry professionals."* Sounds good, right? Industry professionals must be better than a McDonald's accountant.

Even better is they're not hiding themselves. They actually have a

TEAM page you can click on to see their faculty of industry professionals! When you click on that button, you're taken to a page with headshots of all the faculty members. There they are all smiling back at you.

And that's it. Literally just a headshot of ten or twelve random people. No bios, no resumes, no lies, no truth, nothing but their smiling faces.

If you're feeling frustrated, or angry, I get it. How are you supposed to find someone legit to read your work? To tell you if you're on the right track, or completely off? It's not easy. Thing is, it's not supposed to be easy.

A career as a screenwriter is much more difficult than most imagine. Remember the first part of this book? How even folks who got their Club WPS membership cards couldn't hold onto them?

It's really hard.

It takes patience. It takes self-awareness. It takes a certain amount of luck or good fortune. It takes endurance. And it takes a commitment to work at being the best screenwriter you can be.

So, where do you go to find helpful not hurtful feedback on your work?

Find other writers. Join a screenwriting group. Or start one of your own. The pandemic gave us the awareness that most anything can be done virtually. While I suggest you find in-person groups, it's not a requirement. Zoom, Skype, Google, and the rest can all give you a wonderful community of fellow screenwriters.

Before you say it, yes, you're right—feedback from another aspiring screenwriter might be no better (or even worse) than advice from some random reader on some site.

True. But guess what?

YOU'RE NOT PAYING FOR IT!

And . . . you *know* the person. You can see them, speak with them, read *their* work. You know their background, what their level of knowledge is.

Wouldn't you rather get bad notes (for FREE) from some fellow screenwriter who's trying as hard as you are, rather than bad notes (for a price) from some nameless faceless person you've been told is an expert, but may know less than you?

The other important thing about being part of a screenwriters group is you're helping each other, inspiring each other, motivating each other, and holding each other accountable.

We all work harder for other people than we do for ourselves. It's much easier to meet a deadline when you know you must face your group as opposed to simply facing your own reflection.

We're all in this together.

Screenwriting is a lonely, solitary endeavor. Being part of a community is not only good for your writing, but good for your mental health.

Find a group or start your own. Start a *Kill the Dog* Screenwriting Group! And send me a message. Perhaps I'll drop in sometime!

15

GLOSSARY OF INDUSTRY TERMS (REAL AND FAKE)

WHAT FOLLOWS ARE terms from the screenwriting industry. I've also included some terms you hear the gurus and conmen use which are decidedly NOT actual industry terms. Most of the real ones come from television writers rooms, but are used in the feature world as well during notes sessions, etc.

The real ones:

>> *BAIL ON THE PITCH*

Much of a day inside the writers room is filled with writers pitching various ideas. Everything from thoughts on entire episodes, characters and/or their relationships and arcs, villains, plot points, scenes, you name it.

Bailing on a pitch is when a writer is pitching an idea, and halfway through they realize it's a bad idea, or just doesn't work, and they bail on it—meaning they lose all enthusiasm for what they're pitching, and they try to head off impending mockery by insulting themselves or their pitch.

I've heard John Rogers shout across the room to a writer about to bail, *"NEVER bail on the pitch!"*

Bad pitches are part of the gig and often lead to good or even great pitches.

>> *THE CHEADLE*

This one came from the aforementioned John Rogers, probably the best showrunner I've ever worked with. It's when a character onscreen is laughing along with other characters about something, then they turn away and we see their face drop into despair showing their inner turmoil.

It comes from Don Cheadle playing Sammy Davis Jr. in the HBO movie THE RAT PACK. There's a scene where Sammy is going along with a very racist sketch, and everyone is laughing and having fun with it, then Sammy turns away and his face falls, and his anguish is revealed to the audience.

>> *CRAYON VERSION*

I'm proud to say this one comes from my little Pooh brain. If you hear it used anywhere, give a chapeau to me.

It's just another way to say, "bad or weak pitch." Unlike bailing on the pitch, the crayon version is when you know what you are about to pitch is NOT the answer, but it contains the DNA, the anatomy, the bones of what the story needs, so you pitch in the hopes of spurring something better from another writer.

You preface your pitch with, *"Okay, this is the crayon version . . ."* Other variations include *"First draft theater,"* and *"This isn't it, but . . ."*

Clearly, mine is preferred.

>> *HANG A LANTERN ON IT*

When there's a logic issue, or something else isn't working and the writer has exhausted all thoughts as to how to hide the issue, they will sometimes "hang a lantern on it." Meaning, make it a story point. If something doesn't make sense, have the characters talk about it not making sense.

>> *LINE NOT A SONG*

This comes from the world of theater, musical theater to be specific, and it means when something doesn't need as much attention on the page as you think it does. Say a writer advances a story point or character reveal with a four-page scene, when a couple of lines of dialogue would accomplish the same thing.

"*That's a line, not a song.*"

>> *LOGIC COP AND THE FUN TRAIN*

I first heard this on LEVERAGE but don't know the origin. It's basically this: Never let the logic cop stop the fun train. Meaning, don't let a logic issue in your story stop all the fun of the story. The better the story, the less strict logic matters.

>> *THE MAN WITH A HAT*

There are other names for this, but man with a hat is my favorite. It's used to describe when the story comes to a complete halt and a character gives exposition; explaining exactly what happened, what is happening, or what's going to happen. As if a man with a hat just stepped out to speak to the audience.

A writers room example would look like this: the writers are worried about the audience understanding some story point. Someone pitches a solve by having a character explain it away . . . "*Nah, that's just a man with a hat.*"

Why he is wearing a hat, I have no idea.

>> *NOT THE HOUSE NUMBER*

This is in the same neighborhood (see what I did there?) as crayon version. It applies to when a writer is working on a story or character issue and they have an idea that isn't the solve, but it's close—it's in the neighborhood. Meaning, we don't have the house number yet, but we're close; we're on the right street.

>> *ON THE ROOF*

This is specific to TV writers rooms. On the roof is a term used for a character/actor who is close to leaving the show for any number of reasons, but it's not yet public knowledge. Could be the actor is leaving for off screen reasons, could be a character is leaving for story reasons. Whatever it is, in the writers room that character is referred to as being *on the roof.*

It comes from the old joke about the guy who asks his brother to watch his cat while he goes on vacation. After the first day he calls.

TOM: Hey, how's Fluffy doing?
BROTHER: Sorry, Tom, Fluffy's dead.
TOM: What??? Oh my God, now my entire vacation is ruined!
BROTHER: Well, what was I supposed to do, lie to you?
TOM: You could have at least eased me into it. Tell me the cat's gone up on the roof and won't come down. The next time I call you could say Fluffy's still on the roof, but you're trying to find a way to get her down. Then when I call at the end of the week you could say, sorry Tom, but Fluffy tried to jump down or something and she didn't make it, so she's passed on. At least then it wouldn't have been such a shock!
BROTHER: I hear you. I'm sorry.
TOM: It's okay. I'm just sad. Anyway, how's mom?
BROTHER: Mom's on the roof.

>> *THE RAKE (AKA THE ELEPHANTS)*

The rake is usually reserved for comedy rooms, though I have heard it used other places. It refers to something that is really funny, but then goes on so long it's not funny anymore, but then KEEPS going to where not only does it become funny again, it becomes funnier than it was before.

Its origin is a season five episode of THE SIMPSONS where Sideshow Bob steps on a rake that smacks him in the face. He mutters, takes another step and another rake smacks him in the face. He mutters, moves again, and steps on another rake, smacking him in the face yet again. This goes on for a lot of rakes.

Later in the same episode, Bob is lying on the street when a marching band comes through, with all the players stepping on him. Just as he tries to get up, the band is followed by elephants. One by one these elephants continue to appear and step on Bob. Just when you think there's been too many, they keep coming, and it's funny again.

>> *RETREATSPEAK*

This is an evolution of "development-speak" which is the language used by development executives when discussing characters. They'll say "likable" or "relatable." Yuck.

However, Retreatspeak is slightly different. It's when executives have recently returned from one of their annual retreats where they discuss all sorts of things, including how to better communicate with screenwriters.

At each retreat the execs usually get some sort of handout or talking points pamphlet that includes the latest phrases the studios and networks have come up with to toss out during writer meetings. Each year the Retreatspeak is different from the year before because, well, new retreat, new handouts. But when you make the rounds of meetings it's as if all the studios and networks attend the same retreats each year.

Examples of recent Retreatspeak:

- What's the character's takeaway?
- Can we telescope her backstory?
- Are we sure the sister characters pass the circuit test?
- Is the story on brand?

While, I have no clue what most Retreatspeak means (because it means nothing) I do want to take a moment and talk about that last one.

The word BRAND or BRANDING has infiltrated Hollywood like a virus. Branding and Pitch Decks are the new norm because the folks who run the creative side of Hollywood are—in an incredibly ironic and unfortunate twist of fate—not really creative at all, and thus look to whatever is shiny and new, and nothing is newer or shinier than the Tech World.

With so many studios now run by tech companies, the Tech World's vernacular has seeped into the nomenclature of our business as well as into the actual creative development process. And while I understand the argument for it, the argument is wrong.

Words like branding don't belong anywhere near the creative process.

You want to brand yourself as a writer, go for it.

You want to brand yourself as an actor, fine.

You want to brand your network or studio, fine.

I don't recommend doing it, but hey, you're an adult. Unless you use the word adult as a verb, in which case, you're a child.

But we must remember that branding is like structure—it happens *after the fact.*

FX "branded" itself when they put THE SHIELD on the air. And it became a huge hit. Their brand became the network that "pushed the envelope with raw, gritty series."

If THE SHIELD had failed, they likely would still be green lighting shows like SON OF THE BEACH, which was their big success prior to THE SHIELD.

HBO branded itself because of the success of OZ and THE SOPRANOS. Trust me, they tried quite a few other shows, but those weren't nearly as successful, so guess what?

Branding happens.

When you try to stick a Madison Avenue/Silicon Valley notion into an entity that is at its best when imagination and creativity are leading the way, you get a recipe for disaster.

Forget about words like branding and focus on writing.

>> *SANDWICH GUY*

Sandwich Guy is a term created by the amazing writer and showrunner, Barbara Hall. It's a descriptor used to express a portion of the television or movie viewing audience that prefers their stories to be a bit on the simpler side. Not that the shows Sandwich Guy likes aren't complex or intelligent, but rather their concepts are easy for Sandwich Guy to comprehend.

The idea is Sandwich Guy is in the kitchen making his sandwich when his wife asks him from the other room, "*What do you want to watch tonight?*" And Sandwich Guy replies (usually in the timbre of a "lesser educated" individual), "*Let's watch that show where them zombies is eating everyone!*"

Sandwich Guy prefers Broadcast or basic cable series. He doesn't care much for premium cable content. You won't hear Sandwich Guy say, "*Let's watch that show about the cleanup efforts and political and social divarication stemming from the explosion of Reactor number four at the Chernobyl Nuclear Power Plant which caused that Russian inorganic chemist to hang himself!*"

When breaking story in the writers room, the staff will test whether a pitch or plot idea is getting overly complex by asking the room if Sandwich Guy would watch it.

>> *SUCKING ON THE DAY PLAYER CRACK PIPE*

This happens because of exhausted TV writers. When you're writing the same series day after day, episode after episode, season after season—with the same cast of series regulars—it can become a bit tedious at times. That's why it's important to always stay fresh, always be writing stuff for yourself when you're not writing for the show.

Sucking on the day player crack pipe is when a writer inadvertently starts having so much fun writing a new character, they overdo it.

It should be just a day player (that's an actor who comes in for one day's work) having a scene or two with one or more of the regular cast members. The writer is so happy writing someone new, they write WAY too much for this character. The day player becomes more interesting and entertaining than the series regular. Big no-no.

That writer is sucking on the day player crack pipe.

>> *THE TRADES*

The Trades are the trade publications of Hollywood. At one time it was *Variety* and *The Hollywood Reporter*. They are still the old guard of the industry, but now the online source *Deadline* has joined them as well as a couple of lesser entities. *Deadline* is the most popular and well-known now because of its ascension during the paradigm shift when print gave way to electronic publishing.

Here's the thing about the Trades . . . people outside the industry—most of you reading this right now—have this belief that if something is in the Trades then it must be the absolute truth.

Not really.

While I am in no way suggesting what you read isn't true, there's a difference between true and accurate. Watch the brilliant 1981 Sydney Pollack/Kurt Luedtke film ABSENCE OF MALICE for the best example of what I'm talking about.

What those outside the industry don't know about the Trades is that about 80% of all the stories you read about actors, directors, screenwriters, producers, and all the projects happening are what are called "plants." The stories aren't any sort of journalism, they are *planted* in the Trades by agents, managers, PR firms, and the like. They make deals with the Trades (financial and otherwise) to drop stories of their clients and their clients' projects into the pages to create hype and momentum.

I've experienced this firsthand on multiple occasions. When I sold a TV pitch in a big bidding war between multiple networks, we had meetings to determine which Trade publication to put our story in because one of the common deals the Trades make is: if your story gets Page One space, it must be exclusive to that publication. Meaning, what you see on the front page of The Hollywood Reporter will rarely be what's on the front page of Deadline, and so on.

>> *WINONA RYDER*

I think this one is from John Rogers but can't be sure of its origin.

A "Winona Ryder" is bad or unnecessary voice-over, usually overly maudlin or sugary. Comes from Winona Ryder's old woman in EDWARD SCISSORHANDS.

FAKE TERMS USED BY GURUS AND CONMEN

Now we come to some terms I am sure you've all heard from the poseurs out to take your money. They love to use these terms because they sound so pro. What the poseurs don't want you to know is the fact these terms are NOT in any way truthful.

>> SCRIPT DOCTOR

If I had a dime for every time I've heard a charlatan call themselves a "script doctor" I could buy all of us a nice lunch at Hinoki & The Bird.

The term script doctor is a real term in our industry, but . . .

It is a name given to WORKING PROFESSIONAL SCREENWRITERS who are called in to "doctor" scripts that are already in prep or even shooting.

Usually, it's to focus on a specific part of the script. For example, the dialogue or action sequences need doctoring. Or maybe the star wants their character rewritten by a writer they trust. A working professional screenwriter comes in and does a pass—for a fat paycheck—and then goes on their way without taking any screen credit.

Other than working professional screenwriters with a track record of great success, there are NO script doctors in Hollywood.

Let's repeat that:

There are no script doctors in Hollywood.

Anyone calling themselves a *professional script doctor* is lying. Some folks who are referred to as script doctors in our industry include big-time screenwriters such as my friends Randi Mayem Singer (MRS. DOUBTFIRE among many other credits) and Billy Ray (THE HUNGER GAMES, CAPTAIN PHILLIPS, etc.), or Aaron Sorkin (duh), and Phoebe Waller-Bridge (FLEABAG, KILLING EVE, etc.).

Get the point?

There are NO script doctors who don't already have massive screenwriting credits. There are no script doctors you haven't heard of or don't know their work. The only way you become a script doctor is by being a very successful professional screenwriter.

Social media is packed full of folks calling themselves script doctors, yet they have zero or nearly zero credits; nothing you've ever seen or heard of.

Gurus have written How-To books claiming to be professional script doctors. They are lying to you.

I cannot stress this enough—if you have not heard of the person calling themselves a script doctor or don't know their work, they are **not** a script doctor.

>> *SCRIPT CONSULTANT*

If dimes for script doctors could buy us lunch at Hinoki & The Bird, a dime for every "script consultant" could buy us dinner at Nobu. With drinks.

The charlatans love to use terms like script consultant because there's no real way to check whether it's true. There's a famous author of How-To screenwriting books who's made a career out of being a "professional script consultant" yet when you do a deep dive on their actual career, it's Stephen Glass-level embellishment. Anyone can claim they consult on scripts for Paramount or Universal, but unless you talk to the head of Business Affairs and see if checks were actually cut to these folks for said service, there's no way to prove or disprove the claim.

I can save you the time and energy of trying to get the head of BA on the phone . . .

There is no such thing as a script consultant in Hollywood.

The script consultant myth was born out of studio executives going on company retreats and all reading the How-To books. Certain studio executives developed relationships with some of these authors, and probably even discussed a story issue on a particular project over lunch at The Polo Lounge. Said guru then proclaims they are a script consultant to whatever studio the executive works at. Nowadays the moniker has been co-opted by folks on the perimeter of the actual industry (or completely outside of it) in order to inflate their screenwriting expertise. You go to a website or social media account and read about their vast experience as a "professional script consultant" and think they MUST be the real deal.

There are no professional script consultants in Hollywood.

You know who consults on scripts every single day in Hollywood?

Studio executives. Network executives. THEY are the real script consultants. It's part of their job. A big part.

Sometimes they bring in another entity to help them consult on a script. Guess who those folks are?

WORKING PROFESSIONAL SCREENWRITERS.

With membership cards in good standing. And cool jackets.

Being called in to "consult" on a script is the first cousin of being hired as a script doctor. ONLY working professional screenwriters are called in for this.

Studios and producers DO NOT hire people with no screenwriting experience to come in and consultant on, or doctor screenplays they are investing millions of dollars in.

Think of it like this. If YOU were the head of a studio and had a script that needed some professional consultation beyond what your execs have provided—would you bring in someone like Taika Waititi, Craig Mazin or Kelly Marcel? Or would you call in someone with absolutely no experience as a screenwriter and storyteller? Like . . . your dog walker.

BOOM! Callback, baby!

You can see why I rarely write comedy.

The only thing worse than some ass potato calling themselves a script doctor or script consultant is . . . I can barely type this . . .

>> *GHOSTWRITER*

Oh. My. God. Yes, I have come across more than one person calling themselves a professional ghostwriter for Hollywood films and television.

I can't say much here without risking having an embolism, so I will leave it at this . . .

There are no ghostwriters in Hollywood. None. Zero. Not even working professional screenwriters. No such thing as ghostwriters in our industry. If you hear someone claim to be one, don't run . . . call them out. Before that last syllable is out of their mouth, call shenanigans on them. Call bullshit. Call the Show Biz police.

There are no ghostwriters in Hollywood. Only ghosts.

16

WOUND YOUR DARLINGS

I DIDN'T KILL these darlings, merely wounded them. These are *orphans* as we call them in the biz. Random musings that had no clear chapter home but were worth keeping in the book. Some might be repetitive, some might be nuggets of wisdom, but I couldn't bring myself to kill any of them.

- Be honest with yourself and true to yourself. IGNORE all the garbage about rules and Do's and Don'ts, and trust you know how to tell a story.

- The less your brain is filled with rules and inciting incidents and midpoint turns and all the other junk, the more room you will have to fill it with imagination.

- Yet another misconception about screenwriting is that it isn't art, it's just craft.

This is as silly as *you gotta know the rules to break the rules*. Craft and art are indisputably linked. I believe there is no good art without craft.

If art and craft are separate entities existing in their own space without connection to each other, then you're saying the screenplays for MICHAEL CLAYTON, BUTCH CASSIDY AND THE SUNDANCE KID, MOONLIGHT, PULP FICTION, et al. are not art. If that's true then you must believe van Gogh, Pollack, Kahlo, and other artists like them were just throwing paint on the canvas without any knowledge of craft. Because art is art, but craft is craft, right?

Uh, no. Let's take Jackson Pollack since his Drip period is best known by those without much art education. To think Jackson Pollack was simply dripping paint randomly on the canvas with no knowledge of craft—color combinations, composition, broad lines, fine lines, etc.—is simply a completely uninformed opinion.

How about one of my favorite artists of all-time, Jean-Michael Basquiat? When a journalist challenged him that he was not creating art, but simply drawing stick figures, and a child could do what he did, Basquiat responded with *"Every single line means something,"* and proceeded to walk the person through one of his paintings line by line, brushstroke by brushstroke, revealing the composition, the color usage, all the CRAFT stuff.

I have that Basquiat quote on the very computer I'm using to write this book.

You think Gustav Mahler had no expertise in his craft? That he wrote Symphony Number 5 or 9 with no understanding of meter, dynamics, harmony, chord progression, or texture?

My point is you can only create true art once you know your craft. But, BUT . . . the lies you've been fed about what the craft of screenwriting is and isn't must be unlearned. Ignored. Forgotten. There's no special sauce apart from putting in the work, no hack to screenwriting as opposed to prose writing. Or poetry. Or short story writing.

Writing is writing. And when you know the craft, you can create art with your stories, your words. But craft is not inciting incidents and midpoint turns. It's language, syntax, turn of phrase, grammar.

As stated earlier in the book, screenwriting cannot be taught, it can only be learned. The craft of screenwriting can only be learned by writing. And rewriting. You can read all the scripts you want, watch all the films and TV series, and view every YouTube interview with QT or Sorkin, but unless and until you sit down and write, you're never going to learn it.

- Forget all the "structure" talk, and just beat out your story the way it unfolds in your head. Outline it. Outline it again. Use cards on a corkboard, or notes apps, or semaphore flags, or whatever the hell you want to use. Or don't use anything. Write in pencil or pen or magic marker. Type everything on a 1915 Underwood Number 5, or on a Cray Supercomputer. It doesn't matter. What works for you is what's right. I am giving you permission to do it ANY WAY you want. If some guru or professor or charlatan says you can't, or you'll fail, ask them to show you their Club WPS card and cool jacket.

- All the books, gurus, professors, poseurs, wannabes, and even some actual working writers (usually ones who've spent time inside Pixar) can talk all day and night about inciting incidents, midpoint turns, journeying heroes, dark nights of the soul, obstacle-disaster-crisis-climax, rising and falling action, and every other assemblage euphemism, but without QUALITY WRITING, none of it matters. It is a facile theory. You simply cannot write your best if you go at it from these engineering postures.

IT IS NOT CALLED SCREENENGINEERING, IT IS CALLED SCREENWRITING.

- Invest in quality screenwriting software. I believe Fade In Pro is the best, and I have used them all. It's far less expensive than the big-name ones and does far more. And Rian Johnson uses it, so come on!

- Proofread your scripts. Then proofread again. Then find someone or hire someone to proofread before you send out any screenplay. Good writing can be tainted by typos because it shows a lack of care or effort on the writer's part. Look, we all make typos. You've probably found some in this book. But do your very best to clear your work of all typos. Reading a script with a couple of typos isn't a big deal . . . reading a script with six or seven is super annoying. Don't give them any extra reason to say No.

- A. I. The current boogeyman of screenwriters everywhere. Is A.I. going to put us all out of work? If the studios had their way, yes. But not for the reasons you think. It's about money. Not only does A.I. allow them to pay a salary to fewer writers, but there's no health fund, no 401K, no retirement, insurance, none of those other things hiring actual humans forces a company to pay into. Ah, but what they don't know is, it is not a sustainable business model. Because until the reading and viewing public becomes all A.I. themselves, people still want originality, and shared experience, and imagination—things A.I. cannot do. All A.I. is derivative. Despite all the hyperbole and marketing, it cannot *think* for itself. It can merely take in data, process, and export data. All the *thinking* they claim A.I. is capable of is similar to our chapters on structure and Voice . . . it's not what the experts say it is. If you want to keep our creative (and ultimately our everyday) worlds from being taken over by A.I., then demand better from the films and television you watch. Don't settle for just okay. Demand greatness, which can only be achieved by humans. As for worrying or wondering about A.I. during your screenwriting journey, don't. Ignore it. Like you should ignore rope-dangling tabbies.

- Embrace your pain. Every scar is a story.

- Do what Bradbury did and tape a sign above your screen that reads DON'T THINK.

- Don't believe your first draft is good because it's not. If it's finished it's perfect. But it isn't good. Be humble. Write and rewrite, then write some more and rewrite some more.

- Understand that ALL screenwriters, from beginners to Scott Frank, feel at some point during the writing like they are a complete fraud and their idea sucks. Accept it as part of the writer's life and keep pushing through.

- Money spent on experiences such as travel, food, art, music, culture, etc., will help your screenwriting more than any money spent on contests or notes and feedback from people who aren't working professional screenwriters.

- If some non-writing friend, family member, or other entity criticizes your passion or your work, go read Teddy Roosevelt's *Man in the Arena.* Bonus points if you read it aloud to them.

ON SCREENWRITING CONTESTS

Here's the thing. You must be self-aware; you must be honest with yourself about WHY you are entering any contest. If it is for the chance of some agent or producer to discover you and launch your career . . . it's not going to happen. Because all but maybe three or four screenwriting contests are garbage. They exist for one reason: to take your money. They are not in business to help you, despite their altruistic claims. And they can't help you. Even the contests that are considered legitimate by true working professionals are no guarantee anything will happen. The only contests my fellow Club WPS members and I endorse are:

1. The Academy Nicholl Fellowship. It's run by the Academy of Motion Pictures Arts & Sciences and as the name says, it's a fellowship. It doesn't claim grandiose prizes of fame and fortune. Industry professionals pay attention to the winners of Nicholl.

2. The Sundance contests. For the same reason as Nicholl. It's a fellowship which will be much better for your career than winning any of the online contests offering their victors a Zoom with some assistant at a third-tier agency, or meeting with a so-called producer from a production company you've never heard of. And here's the thing . . . the greater the promise the more likely it's a scam. I know of a contest that's been in operation for several years now that PROMISES the winners will have their screenplays financed and made. To date, the closest any winner has come to getting paid or having anything made is a bogus IMDb Pro listing of their project.

3. The Austin Film Festival competition. Not a fellowship, but a contest that's been around forever, has plenty of success stories, and the whole thing is in connection with what is probably the single best film festival in the country. You can tell by the people who attend, and judge, and participate . . . you know their credits, unlike the frauds we covered earlier.

These are the only contests I feel are worth entering if your goal is to help further your career. All the other ones, despite how much online attention they muster, exist to make money and make money only. That includes the one you're thinking of right now. The one I haven't mentioned. The one with the stellar marketing department that has convinced you it's some very special, super connected, super inner-industry think tank incubating the best scripts out there. It ain't.

Haven't you noticed yet that just about everyone who enters these contests always ends up as a quarterfinalist, or semi-finalist, or top ten percent? How can that be? The math makes no sense. How can 90% of the entries finish in the top 10%? Because they want you to keep coming back; to spend more money, to keep entering because you think you were so close last time that maybe this time you'll win!

All that said, my friend Craig T. Williams, a professional screenwriter and producer, opened my eyes to something. Craig entered just about every screenplay contest he could find when he was starting out. He won a lot of them. Not just placed high, won. And not a single one of those victories ever led to anything remotely close to a legitimate Hollywood connection. But Craig wasn't entering to chase that lie. Craig is very self-aware, and he entered those contests for one reason: to give himself confidence. He knew the contests weren't going to help his career, and he knew the judges were likely folks who knew nothing about quality screenwriting, but he did it as a sort of psychological trick on himself. The more accolades he received, the more confident he became, and he was able to translate that confidence into his writing.

Writing with total and complete confidence is one of the greatest strengths a screenwriter can possess. And there is only one way to achieve it; by writing and writing. It happens when you continue to work your butt off and believe in yourself. The more confident your writing, the better and stronger your Voice becomes.

If you want to enter one of the many BS contests online that promise the chance at fame and fortune, go ahead, so long as you're not lying to yourself about what you hope to get out of it.

- Focus on being a screenwriter, not on selling a screenplay.

- Call out charlatans and conmen so others don't fall into their traps.

- Trolls . . . ah, the trolls. Those sad little beings who surf the web looking to drop negativity onto you and your social media world. Ignore them. Remember Teddy R's Man in the Arena. If you are working at this screenwriting thing with your best efforts and best intentions, you are so far ahead of them that they can't even see you.

I've had my share of trolls. People love to bomb into my social media and say no one should listen to my advice because all my credits are "trash," etc.

I never respond with anything other than, *"Thanks for taking the time and energy to comment! Have a blessed day!"* Don't give trolls any of your precious energy. The next time a troll spews their sewage at you, just remember this Truth:

Have you ever met a troll doing better than you?

- When it comes to Tropes and Clichés, people love to say they are the scourge of bad screenwriting, and you should never put them in your screenplays. Here's some truth . . .

  Cliché is not in the idea; it is in the execution. It only becomes cliché if you execute it poorly.

  Tropes are tropes because they are so common. They are so common because we love them. That's how they become tropes. A trope is only "bad" when it is executed poorly.

- There's a very real fear that this book won't sell nearly as well as the ones that have come before it because my message isn't, "Here's the secret!" My message is there is no secret, and you must work harder at this than you ever thought necessary. I believe we're in a culture right now that values doing the least to gain the most. Work ethic is no longer considered a virtue. That said, there are no absolutes. People may succeed by doing the exact opposite of everything this book states. It is not very likely but could happen. Not looking for a hack, shortcut, or secret, and instead putting all your energy into becoming the best screenwriter you can be will not guarantee you any amount of success. But what it WILL guarantee you is exponentially increasing your chances of success.

- Write with complete confidence. BELIEVE IN YOURSELF. But don't be a dick.

- You always hear *"Read scripts, read scripts! That's how you learn."*

  Yes, and . . . don't limit yourself to reading screenplays. Read novels. Read short stories. Read plays. Read essays. Read poetry.

  Read James Baldwin. Read James Lee Burke. Read Flannery O'Connor.

  Read Toni Morrison. Read Lee Child. Read John Cheever.

  Read David Sedaris and David Foster Wallace and David McCullough.

  Read Paul Laurence Dunbar.

  Read Byron and Tennyson and Blake.

  Read Karen Slaughter. Read Robert Crais. Read S.A. Cosby.

  Read Dorothy Parker. Read Roxane Gay. Read Mark Twain.

  Read Maya Angelou. Read Pablo Neruda.

  Read Joan Didion. Read Langston Hughes. Read Haruki Murakami.

  Read Jimmy Breslin and Pete Hamill.

  Read Walter Mosley and Walter Tevis.

  Read Lin-Manuel Miranda. Read Annie Baker. Read Amy Herzog.

  Writing is writing. Just as one cannot write enough, one cannot read enough. As to reading screenplays, I've noticed a trend with the newer generation of up-and-coming screenwriters . . . other than their messiah, QT, they tend to have no frame of screenplay reference prior to the year 2010.

When I'm working with younger screenwriters, they can talk all day long about the MCU, or QT (apparently, he's timeless), or whatever script is the latest flavor of the nanosecond. If that's you, fine, but you are limiting yourself. You are keeping yourself from being as good as you can be.

If you want to give yourself the best chance at success, you must be the best screenwriter you can be. And reading more than the current trends will help that. Seek out great screenplays from the past.

Read Frank Pierson.

Read Charles Brackett, and I.A.L. Diamond (the writers Wilder loved to take credit from).

Read Jay Presson Allen. Read Nancy Dowd. Read Robert Towne.

Read Alvin Sargent. Read Paddy Chayefsky. Read Nora Ephron. Read David S. Ward.

Read Blake Edwards. Read David Mamet.

Read Ernest Lehman. Read Elaine May. Read Paul Mazursky.

Read Robert Benton. Read Bo Goldman. Read Kurt Luedtke.

Read Leigh Chapman. Read Lonne Elder III.

Read Steve Kloves's work before the Harry Potter films.

Read James L. Brooks, and Ron Shelton. Read Richard LaGravenese. Read Naomi Foner.

Read Eric Red, and Eric Hughes, and Eric Roth.

Read Larry Gelbart. Read John Milius. Read Robin Swicord.

Read Gina Prince-Blythewood.

Read Cameron Crowe. Read Billy Ray.

Read Lawrence Kasdan, and Linda Woolverton. Read Barry Jenkins.

And Lord above, please read William Goldman.

- Greg LeMond, one the greatest cyclists in history said, *"Cycling never gets easier; you just go faster."* I believe we can apply this to screenwriting: **It never gets easier; you just get better.** What do I mean by this? I mean it's no easier for me or Scott Frank or Phoebe Waller-Bridge or any other working professional than it is for you. It wasn't easy for Paddy Chayefsky or Madelyn Pugh. Professional screenwriters may write better than you simply because we've been doing it longer. Our screenwriting muscles are in much better shape than someone who's only written one or two things. That doesn't mean you can't pen the greatest screenplay since CHINATOWN on your first try. It's not likely, but it is absolutely possible. So, why not try? And if it isn't great, write another one. And another one. Just please remember, we ALL struggle every time we sit down and type FADE IN. This gig is hard. It's only easy for those who are really bad at it. So, if you're frustrated because you're writing and writing, and it's not getting easier, know the reason for that is because you are getting better with each script, so your bar is being raised again and again.

- Give it everything you have. Whether you are financially supported by a billionaire recluse and have all day and night to write, or whether you're working two jobs to pay rent and feed the five kids you're raising as a single parent, give it everything you have. Find that extra half hour in the morning, or those last forty minutes before bed, find whatever time you can to be disciplined, and write as often as possible. Even if it means sacrificing social media time, or that precious lounging on the couch cuz you just need some "me time." The best use of "me time" is doing something for yourself . . . like becoming a great screenwriter.

  If your significant other or friends or family members don't understand or don't like your commitment, then get a new significant other, new friends, and ignore your family. They'll all come running back when you're nominated. Screenwriting isn't like prose writing, where you can write whenever you feel like it, self-publish whatever you want, and call yourself a "bestseller."

As my good pal Geoffrey Thorne says, "*Screenwriting isn't like book writing. There's a finite number of jobs for an endless number of screenwriters. It's a gladiator ring, and if you don't bring your best Maximus Meridius, you're going to get slaughtered.*"

- Lastly, I want to take time to acknowledge the absolute backbone of the Hollywood industry . . . THE CREW.

  I could not finish this book without giving a shoutout to the unsung heroes of Hollywood. The public hears about directors, actors, producers, and even sometimes writers. But none of those household names would have their giant mansions and overall deals if not for the crews.

  From craft service to makeup and hair, to drivers, to grips and sparkers, to camera operators and Steadicam heroes, to focus pullers and loaders, to sound mixers and boomers, to ADs and Set PAs, to editors, to script supervisors, to wardrobe and props assistants, to greens, to caterers, to stunt badasses and armorers, to special effects freaks, and casting associates, to office PAs, to all the coordinators, to security guards, to the background players and my own family, 2ND TEAM! And to every other crew member ever, you are truly the ones who make the magic of movies and television come to life.

  Thank you.

17

THE ABBY SINGER

BOOK RECOMMENDATIONS

"Hey, Guyot, so you clearly hate all books on screenwriting!"

No. Just the ones spewing bad How-To advice from folks who don't have informed opinions.

I love books on writing. Note I said "writing" not "screenwriting." Because, as mentioned previously, one of the lies the gurus and charlatans try to convince you of is that screenwriting is not the same as actual writing.

It is in fact exactly the same. Think of it this way . . .

There are sprinters in the Olympics and there are marathoners. Two very different disciplines, but both are runners. You cannot say sprinters are not runners any more than you can say marathoners are not runners.

Screenwriting is writing.

I love writers. I love writing. I love books on writing written by writers. And there are several that I highly recommend. From the man who taught us all—William Goldman—to the greatest unpublished writer in history—Snoopy—here is a list of some of the books I believe will help you on your journey more than any How-To screenwriting book (except this one).

Enjoy!

THE WAR OF ART

Steve Pressfield

I'm on record as saying this is the best book on writing I've ever read. Note how I didn't say The Best Ever. It's the best *I've read*. This book is so short it's almost a pamphlet. You can read the entire thing in the morning and still make it to your lunch at SoHo House. Yet, Pressfield has filled its pages with more direct, honest, no-holds-barred, critical information on the most important part of the successful writer's life: mindset.

Pressfield makes a compelling case that the War of Art is our battle with Resistance; a three-dimensional, multi-headed, shape-shifting monster that is coming at our imagination, inspiration, and motivation with a force greater than that of Tsar Bomba, to keep us from creating. You must know your enemy to defeat your enemy.

MAKING MOVIES

Sidney Lumet

One of the greatest directors Hollywood has ever known, and a darn fine screenwriter as well, Sidney Lumet's book is a Masterclass in the eponymous craft. Not only does he walk you through nearly every single aspect of movie making, but he manages to drop in some wonderful True Hollywood tales, as well as give his insights on storytelling for the visual medium that are second to none. Sidney was incredibly generous to me when I knew him, and his generosity shines in this book. Anyone who wants to be part of the film industry in any way, from craft service to studio CEO, will benefit from this book.

IN THE BLINK OF AN EYE

Walter Murch

My buddy, the director Walter Hill, once told me, "*You always make three movies: the movie you write, the movie you shoot, and the movie you edit.*" The legendary Walter Murch is one of the best to do that last part. The man has 13 Oscar and BAFTA nominations, winning four times. His book is "about" editing (note the quotation marks), but it's really one of the most penetrating books about storytelling I've read. Every screenwriter I know who's read this book has said they are better for it.

ON WRITING

Stephen King

One could not compile any list of great books on writing without including the granddaddy of them all. I would bet heavily that if you polled 1000 writers on what is the best book on writing, 950 of them will tell you this one. The first half is the origin story of one of our greatest scribes, and the second half may be the finest practical guide to writing ever put to page.

WRITING FOR LOVE AND/OR MONEY

Frank Gilroy

I love this book, and it's never included in any discussions about books on writing. Frank Gilroy is the father of two of the best screenwriters working today—Tony and Dan Gilroy. A playwright and screenwriter, Frank won the Tony, the Pulitzer, the Obie, The Silver Bear, and on and on. This book is a compilation of the journals he kept during his amazing career. It's filled with the high moments, but what's more captivating are the low moments; when he lost jobs, when his work received bad reviews, and when the money ran out. It's one of the most vulnerable, honest looks into what it really takes to live the writer's life.

ADVENTURES IN THE SCREEN TRADE

William Goldman

The Bible. Written by the Jesus of screenwriting, William Goldman. One of the best to ever type FADE IN: and this memoir of his time in the trenches of Hollywood is an absolute must-read for anyone considering a career as a screenwriter. Though published more than forty years ago, the information, anecdotes, advice, and instruction Goldman shares are as relevant today as the day the book came out.

BONUS: read this, then his follow-up, *Which Lie Did I Tell?*

SCULPTING IN TIME

Andrey Tarkovsky

If you don't recognize the name, Tarkovsky is widely considered one of the best filmmakers by the people *you* consider to be the best filmmakers. The book is both incredibly dense and thoroughly enjoyable. Reading it is like attending a private session with a Master of Visual Storytelling.

WHAT I TALK ABOUT WHEN I TALK ABOUT RUNNING

Haruki Murakami

One of the most important writers of the last half-century, Murakami is not a screenwriter. And this book was originally going to be a journal about training for long-distance running. But a funny thing happened on the way to the start line. Murakami's writer soul took over. Yes, the book's focus is running, but it's really about *being* a writer. You won't find any inciting incident blather here, but you will find something to make you a better screenwriter.

SNOOPY'S GUIDE TO THE WRITING LIFE

Barnaby Conrad

My hero. It is not hyperbole when I say it was Snoopy who first made me want to become a writer. Growing up, I was a devout reader of *Peanuts*, and whenever the strip featured Snoopy and his quest to become the world's greatest novelist, something spoke to me. I wanted what Snoopy wanted. This book is a compilation of all the Peanuts strips to feature Snoopy and his trusty typewriter and contains commentary from some of our greatest human writers. I have probably read it cover to cover at least a half dozen times.

18

THE MARTINI SHOT

CONGRATULATIONS! YOU ARE clearly dedicated to improving your abilities and chances of success. Or maybe you just had an afternoon to kill. Either way, I'm glad you're still with me.

We've had a lot of fun at the expense of some decent human beings who were probably only trying to pay the rent. I get it. I've been there. But as mentioned, not telling you the truth will not help you get better.

If you've read up to this point, you are already a better screenwriter. Or I should say, you could be . . . if you were paying attention and absorbing the message of this book.

As mentioned, the reason for this book is to help you. Being a working professional screenwriter is a fantastic life. An absolute blessing of a job if you love making up stories.

I love storytelling. And I love storytellers.

Faith has been a huge part of my success. I have faith in God and owe all my success to Him. But even if you don't believe in the whole SkyDaddy thing, I think it's important for screenwriters to have faith in something . . . anything.

Faith and writing go together like mac & cheese, Paul & Joanne, Sacco & Vanzetti, Calvin & Hobbes . . . you get the picture.

Have faith in *something*. If not a higher power, then in yourself. In Story. In Art. In the belief that the world needs creatives now more than ever.

I would love to hear from you. Hear about your screenwriting journey, and if anything in this book helped you. Even if you hated the book, let me know. I always want to get better.

There are some things in my life which are connected to my screenwriting. Or at least things that have taught me lessons I've applied to my life as a screenwriter.

Golf. A game that inspires true passion and true frustration. A game I can hate with every fiber of my being while never ceasing to love it with all my heart.

Cycling. Riding my bike has saved my life, literally. Yes, I'm using literally correctly. I, like so many writers in history, have battled mental health and depression to the point of suicidal thoughts. The bike has saved me. Riding a bike has such a kinship to writing, yet I can't put it into words. I guess it has to do with pushing oneself, exceeding the limits of what you thought you were capable of, and those rare times I call the flow state: when all is right, and you know you are exactly where you're supposed to be doing exactly what you were put here to do, and doing it as well as you can . . . until you do it better the next time.

I thought long and hard about how I wanted to end this book. What I wanted to leave you with. And since the theme, the essence, the core of this book is about truth, I feel that's what I should leave you with. So, here is your final, undisputed, irrefutable TRUTH . . .

You are better than you think you are.

You can do more than you think you can.

Now go write. And mention me in your acceptance speeches.

FADE OUT

ALWAYS READ THE CREDITS!

WITHOUT THESE PEOPLE, THIS BOOK WOULD NOT EXIST.

First and foremost, Gregg Gellman, a man who not only has never abandoned me but has been there on my darkest days as well as my brightest ones. I am forever in your debt.

The lovely staff at Le Buzz Plaza Palomino for all the coffee and support, and for letting me commandeer that spot in the corner all those months.

Geoffrey Thorne, friend and brother. I could not have made it through the last few years, let alone written this book, without you being there.

David & Maili Montgomery, for 20+ years of friendship and incredible generosity. Proverbs 17:17.

Rachel Lithgow for that first read and encouragement.

Melissa Stephens for your generosity, mad skills, and the Farrell's memories.

Barbara and Karen Hall for teaching me how to be a professional writer.

John Rogers for the friendship and countless lessons.

Brian Koppelman for being the first one to call after *GEOSTORM*, and for always reminding me of what's truly important in this thing we do.

Craig Mazin for treating me like a friend even though we hardly knew each other.

Dennis Palumbo for saving me. Matt Reeves for not saving me.

Craig T. Williams and Bart Baker, my screenwriting brothers, who were there when the idea for this book was born.

Desi Aragon for all your creative energy. And Jaz Garewal for bringing us together.

Bryon Quertermous for the Scrivener education, and long emails between writer friends.

Chow Yun-Fat for threatening to fire me.

Keith Snyder for making it come to life.

Scott Rosenberg, Shane Black, Jay Presson Allen, Blake Edwards, Tony Gilroy, Nancy Dowd, John Milius, Theodore Witcher, Billy Ray, William Goldman, et al. for the inspiration and pushing me to always be better.

Finally, to the painter, Michelle Monteleone, who not only gave me the title for this book, but made the writing of it possible, spiritually and emotionally. It's yours as much as mine.

SCREENWRITINGTRUTH.COM